D1599296

MASTERS OF THE OCCULT

Also by Daniel Cohen

A MODERN LOOK AT MONSTERS

MYSTERIOUS PLACES

MYTHS OF THE SPACE AGE

For Younger Readers

TALKING WITH THE ANIMALS

THE AGE OF GIANT MAMMALS

SECRETS FROM ANCIENT GRAVES

MASTERS OF THE OCCULT

By DANIEL COHEN

ILLUSTRATED

DODD, MEAD & COMPANY
NEW YORK

ISBN 0-396-06407-8
Library of Congress Catalog Card Number: 74-165669

Printed in the United States of America
by the Cornwall Press, Inc., Cornwall, N.Y.

To Frank and Jayne Stelle

INTRODUCTION

The Leaders and the Led

A FEW YEARS AGO I wrote about what I called "the occult underground." I contended that there were an enormous number of people who held wildly unconventional and downright bizarre beliefs. However, the importance and widespread hold of such beliefs was usually ignored by serious students of American society. The believers in the occult were brushed aside as "the lunatic fringe."

Well, since that time the occult underground has surfaced—with a bang. Everything from astrology to witchcraft is booming, and critics who once ignored occultism are now seriously concerned that its growth is another sign that America is going mad.

One often hears the claim advanced by both the occultists and their enemies that occultism is enjoying its greatest boom in three or four hundred years. We are now, it is said, entering "the Age of Aquarius." Science and rationalism are out and the occult is in. The claim is both hysterical and unhistoric. One need only look back at the burgeoning spiritualist movement of the late nineteenth century to see that Americans held a lot of strange ideas at that time. Then too, one heard the warnings that we were going mad. But still it would be shortsighted to ignore this new wave of interest in the occult.

What is occultism? The word occult itself originally means hidden or secret and the word is a good one. All of those subjects that have been lumped under the heading of occult concern powers or phenomena that are supposedly hidden or secret. None of these powers or phenomena are testable by means that could reasonably be defined as scientific. Though some modern occultists say that their powers have been "scientifically proved," this is just idle chatter.

It is not that any form of occultism has become more scientifically respectable, rather it is that science itself has become less respectable. Over the last few years a lot of people, particularly young people have become profoundly disappointed in science, and hostile toward it. What better way to express anger than to adopt beliefs that are thoroughly and blatantly unscientific.

In view of the now painfully obvious fact that we are living in the midst of an occult explosion it might be useful to take a look at some of those masters of occult movements of the past and present.

Leaders are vital because all forms of occultism are profoundly despotic in character. There is no such thing as a democratic occult movement—there can't be. The whole idea of occultism presupposes that there are individuals who possess knowledge or powers that ordinary mortals do not possess. Occasionally these masters of the occult may choose to enlist disciples whom they will train. But the training process is traditionally a long, torturous, and highly secret one. It is rarely completed successfully. In general, occult powers seem nontransferable, and few occult movements long survive the death of their founder. In the case of occult scholars the secret knowledge that they obtained always seems to be lost immediately after their death.

The masters of the occult themselves are often fascinating and enigmatic individuals, even though they do not possess the powers they claim. Attempting to unravel their tangled lives and characters, and form some sort of intelligent judgments about them, has proved to be a stimulating, though often frustrating task.

Throughout history there have been thousands of individuals who might have been labeled masters of the occult. I've been chosen to explore the histories of a mere handful. The choice has been an entirely personal one. Some individuals like Madame Blavatsky and John Dee would almost certainly be included in anybody's list of occult masters. Some like Cagliostro and Rasputin have been covered so often, another treatment of them hardly seems necessary. Still others, like Edgar Cayce and Jeane Dixon I find rather dull as personalities, no matter how many followers they may have, so I have not included them.

Theosophists and scientologists are not going to like what I have to say about Madame Blavatsky or L. Ron Hubbard, the respective founders of those movements. Those who believe in psychic phenomena will think that I have given D. D. Home and Eileen Garrett short shrift. In general those attracted to occult subjects will assume I am blinded by outdated materialism, and that I suffer from the credulity of incredulity. I won't argue the point.

But I must utter a word of warning to those who are not theosophists, scientologists, psychic buffs, or any other form of occultist. It is all too easy to stand back and denounce the occult leaders as a bunch of frauds and nuts, and their followers as poor deluded fools, who perhaps get no better than they deserve.

Such a harsh and offhand judgment misses the point. In fact, most of the occult masters are not crazy, and are either only partially frauds, or not conscious frauds at all. And they do possess real power—not the power to raise the dead or see the future but the power to influence people, to make people believe them, and perhaps to make them believe themselves.

The followers of the occult masters are often intelligent and reasonable people for whom the occult master fills a deep and important need.

Simply dismissing with scorn the beliefs—however odd they may seem—that are held by large numbers of people is itself rather foolish, and a bit dangerous. For example, one day a friend of yours, who is not crazy or stupid, will begin telling you about this wonderful new group that he has just joined. The ideas of this group may sound a bit odd, but your friend surely would never be taken in by one of those weird cults. And so you say to yourself, perhaps this one is different, perhaps they really do have something this time . . .

Contents

Illustrations

Following page 110

MASTERS OF THE OCCULT

CHAPTER I

Mythical Masters

IN THE YEAR 1614 a very remarkable pamphlet was published in the town of Cassel in Germany. Like all pamphlets of the day it had a very long title—*The Fama of the Fraternity of the Meritorious Order of the Rosy Cross Addressed to the Learned in General and the Governors of Europe.*

The author or authors of *The Fama,* as the pamphlet came to be known were anonymous. They claimed to be a group of adepts belonging to a secret and mysterious order of the Rosy Cross. Much of *The Fama* concerns the life of the founder of the order, a man known only as C.R.C. Later documents identified C.R.C. as Christian Rosenkreuz or, in a Latinized version, Christianus Rosae Crucis, hence the initials C.R.C.

According to *The Fama* Rosenkreuz was a Dutchman born in 1378. At the age of four he was placed in a monastery, but while still a boy he set out on a pilgrimage to Jerusalem with a monk. The monk died along the way and Rosenkreuz went on to Damascus, where his skill in medicine made him a popular figure. He then proceeded to the city of "Damcar" (though this city was supposed to be in Arabia it has never been located and is probably mythical).

"Damcar" was a city of wise men "to whom Nature was discovered." It seems that the wise men had been expecting Rosenkreuz. They taught him Arabic, physics, and mathematics, and most importantly introduced him to the mysterious *Book M,* which contained the secrets of the universe. Rosenkreuz translated *Book M* into Latin. He traveled around the Middle East learning science, magic, and mysticism. Finally he felt able to return to Europe and teach men how to "order all their studies on those sure and sound foundations."

Upon his return to Germany, Rosenkreuz began to compose a book which contained "whatsoever can be desired or hoped for by man." In this project he was aided by seven monks from the monastery in which he had been placed as a boy. When the book was completed Rosenkreuz and his associates realized that the world was not ready for the knowledge it contained. The eight thus decided to form the secret order called the Fraternity of the Rosy Cross. They were to go to different countries where they were to influence subtly and secretly the learned and powerful. Each year the members of the order were to return to Germany for a meeting, and each member was to nominate a successor before he died. They also swore to keep their organization secret for at least a century.

Rosenkreuz himself finally died in 1484—at the age of one hundred and six—and was buried in a large tomb, a secret one naturally. After all the original members of the group died, the location of Rosenkreuz's tomb was forgotten, and was rediscovered only by accident by members of the third generation of adepts who were rebuilding one of their secret dwellings.

Over a sealed door were the words, "I shall open after 120

years." Inside was a seven-sided vault that was lighted by a mysterious eternally burning light. In the center of the vault was an altar, and underneath the altar was the body of Rosenkreuz himself, "whole and unconsumed." There were also a number of magical objects, and a document called *Book T*, which was described as "our greatest treasure next to the Bible."

It was the discovery of the tomb that inspired the members of the Fraternity of the Rosy Cross, who were to become known as Rosicrucians, to issue the first public notice of their existence. The Rosicrucians appealed to all worthy and learned men to join their fraternity. But joining wasn't an easy thing to do. The only way for a person to join was to publish his interest in a public letter and wait for some member of the society to contact him.

The Fama ended with the assurance that all members of the fraternity were good Lutherans, and with a denunciation of alchemy, despite the fact that much of *The Fama* is couched in the obscure and mystical symbolism common to alchemical writing.

The Fama created considerable excitement, particularly among the mystically minded scholars of Germany. Quite a number published their desire to join the mysterious fraternity, but as far as we can tell no one was ever contacted.

In 1615, a year after *The Fama* appeared, another Rosicrucian document, *The Confession of the Fraternity of Rosae Crucis,* was published. This document gave more details about the group and was more aggressively pro-Lutheran and anti-Catholic. The Rosicrucians were getting ready to take over Europe, it said, and *The Confession* expressed the pious hope that they would put an end to the Pope's "asinine braying" by tearing him to pieces with nails.

The following year the third of the original Rosicrucian manifestos appeared, *The Chemical Wedding of Christian Rosenkreuz. The Chemical Wedding* was the first of the documents in which the full name of the founder of the Rosicrucians was revealed, and in many ways it is the oddest of the three documents. The book concerns a mythical king and queen who are married in a bizarre ceremony in which Rosenkreuz is a witness. The book contains enough sexual symbolism to delight any Freudian. Some have seen *The Chemical Wedding* as a satire on the other Rosicrucian writings, but it is quite typical of much of the alchemical-mystical writing of the time. It suggests that alchemy is not so much the transmutation of base metals into gold, but the regeneration of the human soul. This was a fairly common idea. However, the Rosicrucian documents do mention, in an offhand sort of way, that the order possessed more riches than all the kings in the world.

Violently pro- and anti-Rosicrucian pamphlets were published, and many waited hopefully to be contacted by the secret adepts, and initiated into the fraternity. But nothing else happened, and by 1620 interest in Christian Rosenkruez's secret order of adepts had faded, temporarily.

The whole story of Christian Rosenkreuz, his adventures and his secret society, sounds like a melodramatic romance, which is exactly what it was. Most modern scholars believe that the Rosicrucian documents were written, at least in part, by a Lutheran deacon named Johann Valentin Andreä. Andreä actually confessed to being the author of *The Chemical Wedding,* in his autobiography. The rose and the cross symbols of the order were also contained in Luther's seal and in Andreä's family coat of arms.

Why were the Rosicrucian manifestos published at all? Some believe that there really was some sort of ancient Rosicrucian society, but most non-occult scholars reject this theory because there is simply no hard evidence to support it. Perhaps Andreä and his friends wished to start a Lutheran secret society. In his youth Andreä was an unorthodox Lutheran, and might just have been the kind of man to entertain such a project. The Rosicrucian manifestos would then have been designed to interest like-minded Lutherans, without giving away too much about the founders of the group. If this was the case the society never got off the ground. A few members may have been initiated, in secret, though there is no evidence of this.

Others have speculated that the Rosicrucian manifestos are primarily anti-Catholic propaganda, or that they are simply a broad satire, ridiculing alchemical and mystical ideas. The real reasons behind the creation of the Rosicrucian manifestos are now lost beyond recall. But whatever they were—the Lutheran-Catholic dispute, alchemy, fifteenth-century mysticism—they have no relevance to today's world. Yet, in name at least, Rosicrucianism has flourished for over three hundred and fifty years. One can hardly pick up a publication in America today without encountering an ad urging you to join the ancient and mystic brotherhood of the Rosicrucians, and share in the secret wisdom of the ages.

Of course today's Rosicrucians are in no way direct descendants of the fifteenth-century Rosicrucians, if indeed there were any. Numerous diverse groups bearing the name Rosicrucian have appeared through the years. Modern Rosicrucians make claims for their organization which make the claims of the original Rosicrucian manifestos sound like sober realism. But the mere fact that a modern occult group chooses to call itself Rosicrucian (actually there are several competing Rosicrucian groups today) is an indication of the enormous and continuing appeal of the story of Christian Rosenkreuz.

Rosenkreuz is the perfect Master of the Occult. His life is

cloaked in mystery. What he says and what is said about him are deliberately enigmatic and obscure. He is willing to share his secrets with a small and select group. His followers disdain wealth and power, and indicate that their mission is a spiritual one, yet it is broadly hinted that a true disciple can obtain all the wealth and power he could wish for.

The magic words and ceremonies, all the secret mumbo-jumbo, are almost childishly elaborate, yet for several hundred years now many people, by no means all of them fools, have believed in one form or another of Rosicrucianism, and have sought to discover, in the entirely mythical life of Christian Rosenkreuz, truths that would help illuminate their own lives.

Much of the language and outlook of the early Rosicrucian manifestos, indeed of all occult literature, up until the late eighteenth century was based upon alchemy. There were many, many real alchemists who had reputations for working all manner of marvels, and we shall meet a few of them in later chapters. But the history of alchemy also contains an impressive number of mythical and legendary masters—that is, individuals who either were entirely imaginary or may have been real, but whose marvelous alchemical deeds are imaginary. Moses was supposed to have been a pioneer alchemist. Even more important was Moses' sister Miriam, who was also known as Maria the Jewess, or under the Christianized title Maria Prophetissa. In fact there really may have been a famous woman alchemist named Maria in the early years of the Christian era. A lot of alchemical theory is also wrongly attributed to Plato and Cleopatra, who did exist, and to the Egyptian goddess Isis, who did not.

But surely the most august figure in the history of alchemy, indeed one of the most respected and awesome figures in all occult history is Hermes Trismegistus, and his fame seems due largely to a misunderstanding.

It was common for the Greeks to identify their own gods with those of other nations. They identified their god Hermes with the ancient Egyptian god Thoth or Tehuti, the god of wisdom. Hermes Trismegistus simply means "Hermes Thrice Powerful," because in Egyptian writings Thoth is often referred to as "twice very great" or even "five times very great." Since Thoth was the god of wisdom many works were attributed to him. The Greeks considered Egypt the home of most magical knowledge. Modern occultists retain this exaggerated view of Egyptian magic.

Somewhere around the fourteenth or fifteenth century the true origin of the name Hermes Trismegistus was forgotten, and it was believed that the name belonged to an ancient king or sage of Egypt. All manner of works, magical, mystical, astrological, and particularly alchemical were ascribed to him. The whole body of works, which came to be called Hermetic, had an enormous influence on Renaissance thinkers.

One of the things about the Hermetic writings that most impressed scholars of the fifteenth and sixteenth centuries was that far from conflicting with Christian doctrine, the writings of this ancient Egyptian sage actually seemed to confirm it. This was hardly surprising since most of the Hermetic writings were actually composed by heretical Christian sects during the first few centuries of the Christian era.

Probably the most influential document ever ascribed to the mythical Hermes was the *Tabula Smaragdina* or *Emerald Tablet*. It was reputed to have been discovered by Alexander the Great or Sarah, the wife of Abraham, or the magician Apollonius of Tyana, inscribed on a slab of emerald in the tomb of Hermes Trismegistus. The *Emerald Tablet* is supposed to summarize the principles of change in Nature, and thus is the basis of much alchemical speculation. From it you can get some of the flavor of the Hermetic writings:

> True it is, without falsehood, certain and most true. That which is above is like to that which is below, and that which is below is like to that which is above, to accomplish the miracles of one thing.
>
> And as all things were by the contemplation of one, so all things arose from this one thing by a single act of adaptation.
>
> The father thereof is the Sun, the mother the Moon.
>
> The Wind carried in its womb, the Earth is nurse thereof.
>
> It is the father of all works of wonder throughout the whole world.
>
> The power thereof is perfect.
>
> If it be cast onto Earth, it will separate the element of Earth from that of fire, the subtle from the gross.
>
> With great sagacity it doth ascend gently from Earth to Heaven.
>
> Again it doth descend to Earth, and uniteth in itself the force from things superior and things inferior.
>
> Thus thou wilt possess the glory of the brightness of the whole world, and all obscurity will fly far from thee.
>
> This thing is the strong fortitude of all strength, for it overcometh every subtle thing and doth penetrate every solid substance.
>
> Thus was the world created.
>
> Hence there will be marvelous adaptations achieved, of which the manner is this.
>
> For this reason I am called Hermes Trismegistus, because I hold three parts of the wisdom of the whole world.
>
> That which I had to say about the operation of Sol is completed.

If the meaning of the *Emerald Tablet* escapes you, you are in good company. Medieval and Renaissance scholars wrote weighty tomes attempting to explain it, and discover what "the thing" is. None succeeded.

The exact origins of the celebrated *Emerald Tablet* are lost, but it is certainly not nearly as old as it is supposed to be. The content of the *Emerald Tablet* can be traced back, with a fair degree of certainty, to Moslem alchemists in Syria in about the tenth or eleventh centuries. The Moslems said that Noah took the *Emerald Tablet* with him on the Ark.

What does it mean? In a sort of a general way the *Emerald Tablet* seems to state the ancient principles of sympathetic magic, and as such is not a particularly useful document.

Yet even after the mythical quality of Hermes Trismegistus became known, and the origins of the Hermetic writings traced, they continued to cast a hypnotic spell over occultists, and they still do. Wrote G. R. S. Mead, an early twentieth-century occultist:

"The more one studies the best of these mystical sermons, casting aside all prejudices, and trying to feel and think with the writers, the more one is conscious of approaching the threshold of what may well be believed to have been the true adytum of the best in the mystery traditions of antiquity. Innumerable are the hints of the greatness and immensities lying beyond that threshold—among other precious things the vision of the key to Egypt's wisdom the interpretation of apocalypsis by the light of the sun-clear epopoeia of the intelligible cosmos."

". . . Hints of the greatness and immensities lying beyond that threshold . . ." Surely that is one of the most powerful lures that the masters of the occult have held out to their followers.

While the average reader may never have heard of Christian Rosenkreuz or Hermes Trismegistus, he has certainly heard of that most celebrated of all occult masters, Faust. Yet Faust too was mythical, or it might be more accurate to say legendary, for it seems that there really was a Faust. But the Faust of legend resembles the historical Faust in name only.

There are a few brief contemporary references to a Johann Faust, an early sixteenth-century German magician. He is generally described as a charlatan and a fool. There is nothing in the scanty historical record to indicate that Johann Faust in any way stood out above the horde of other crooked magicians of his time. Yet he must have had a certain flamboyance that attracted attention, for after his death he came to be regarded as the archetype of the magician, sorcerer, and occultist.

Men of the sixteenth century were of two minds about magic. On the one hand, as good Christians they knew that the study of ancient and obscure documents should not give one special powers, since all of these powers had to be conferred by God. Surely there was no hidden knowledge that should allow men to perform miracles without God's permission. Besides most of these occult documents were either pagan or heretical and therefore thoroughly evil.

On the other hand, people did believe in magic. So they decided that the magicians did not get their power from the study of ancient spells and formulas, but rather they obtained it directly from the Devil. The spells and formulas were really only means of directing the Devil's power. All magic was evil and all magicians servants of Satan. Such beliefs about magic were particularly strong in Lutheran Germany, and they all came to rest upon the obscure Johann Faust.

One of the first legendary biographies of Faust appeared in

1587. According to this book the magician had spent years studying the works of the ancients, and on one dark night he retired to a forest, drew magical figures upon the ground, uttered secret incantations and summoned up the Devil.

"Why am I called, and what is your command?" asked His Satanic Majesty. Faust asked the Devil to do his bidding, and the Devil agreed, but he would serve the magician only for a period of twenty-four years. After that, he would claim Faust "body and soul." The pact between Faust and the Devil was signed in blood.

Aided by the Devil, Faust proceeded to astonish the world. His particular specialty seemed to be necromancy—summoning up the spirits of the dead for the amazement or amusement of kings and princes.

Faust started as a seeker of forbidden occult wisdom, but as time went on he became more evil and depraved. The night before his pact was to run out Faust held a huge banquet for all of his friends. He announced that this was the last day of his life, and explained how he had received his powers. Then he retired to his bedroom to await the end. A furious storm erupted, but the sounds of thunder were more than matched by the awful sounds coming from the magician's bedroom. No one had the courage to go into the room to see what was happening. The next morning Faust's horrified friends found his hideously mangled body in a field outside the house.

Many writers, including Goethe, have used the Faust story, as a basis for books, plays, and operas. Hardly surprising, since it is a marvelous story. And that is perhaps one final reason why the masters of the occult continue to fascinate us —they are the stuff of marvelous stories.

CHAPTER II

Cornelius Agrippa

Of the many stories told about the great Renaissance scholar, scientist, and sorcerer Cornelius Agrippa, this is perhaps the most extraordinary.

While he was residing at the university city of Louvain, Agrippa had to leave his house, and he knew that he would be gone for some time. He gave the key to his study to his wife, but warned her that under no circumstances was anyone to be allowed to enter the room, for that was the room where the wizard kept all his magical implements and manuscripts.

Agrippa's wife was notably uncurious about her husband's magic. But the attic of the house had been rented out to a young student who burned with a fierce desire to see the forbidden room. He thought that if he could gain entrance to this room he might be able to learn the secret, supposedly possessed by Agrippa, of turning base metals into gold.

The youth was handsome and eloquent, and had little trouble in persuading Agrippa's wife to turn over the key. But she ordered him not to remove anything from the room and he promised to obey.

When the student entered the forbidden study the first thing to catch his eye was a large *grimoire* or book of magical spells that lay open on Agrippa's desk. The youth sat down and began to read aloud. At the first word he thought he heard a knock at the door, but deciding that it was his imagination he went on reading aloud. There was another knock which startled the student right out of his chair. He tried to say, "Come in," but was too frightened to speak.

The door opened slowly and a large scowling stranger entered. "Why was I summoned?" demanded the stranger.

"I did not summon you," said the trembling student.

"You did," said the stranger, advancing menacingly, "and the demons are not to be invoked in vain."

At this the student was again frightened into speechlessness. The demon was now thoroughly enraged that this boy should call him up on what seemed a mere whim, so he seized the unfortunate youth by the throat and choked the life out of him.

When Agrippa returned home a few days later, he found his house overrun by demons. "Some of them were sitting on the chimney pots, kicking up their legs in the air; while others were playing at leapfrog on the very edge of the parapet. His study was so filled with them that he found it difficult to make his way to his desk . . ."

When Agrippa spied the open book on his desk and the dead student on the floor he immediately guessed what had happened. The magician quickly dismissed all the minor demons who were crowding around and confronted the principal demon. Why, asked Agrippa, had the demon been so rash and foolish to kill the boy? The demon insisted that the presumptuous youth had deserved death for calling him up without good reason. Agrippa was not mollified and spoke sharply to the demon.

The student's murder had presented Agrippa with a problem. His magical activities had already made him unpopular in Louvain, and now with an unexplained dead body in his house, he would surely be accused of murder. In order to provide himself with the perfect alibi Agrippa ordered the demon to reanimate the corpse and walk around with it in the marketplace, so that everyone would believe that the student was alive, while Agrippa was at home.

The demon did as ordered. Murderer and corpse walked through the marketplace arm in arm for the entire afternoon. At sunset the body fell down cold and lifeless. It was rushed to the hospital, but of course there was no reviving the young man a second time. The general opinion was that the youth had died of a sudden apoplectic stroke. But when the body was examined more closely the marks of strangulation were found on the neck, and the claw marks of the demon on other parts of the body. Then there was a story that the youth's odd companion had vanished in a puff of smoke shortly after the boy collapsed.

The townsfolk managed to piece together the story, so that despite his attempts at deception, Agrippa was forced to flee Louvain.

This macabre, but charming tale is so fantastic that it is difficult to believe that anyone ever took it for more than a fable. Yet it was recorded quite seriously by the Jesuit scholar, Martin Antoine Del Rio, in his book on magic and demonology, published in Louvain in 1599. The book was extremely popular and influential. Del Rio himself was no mere superstitious scribbler. On the contrary, he was an extraordinarily well-educated man, but one who accurately reflected the beliefs and prejudices of his own time. One of those beliefs was that Agrippa was a wizard in league with the Devil.

Henry Cornelius Agrippa von Nettesheim was born at Cologne on the fourteenth of September, 1486. He was educated at the University of Cologne, and as a young man served as a soldier in the army of Maximilian I of Germany.

While still in his early twenties, Agrippa had acquired a reputation for being a skilled alchemist. (It was widely rumored that he had actually found the long-sought-after Philosopher's Stone.) Agrippa was also a respected and learned astrologer in a time when astrologers abounded. But the occult arts were not his only accomplishments. Melanchthon, the great German religious reformer, spoke of Agrippa with respect, and the celebrated Erasmus echoed this respect. But the man who surpassed all in praise of Agrippa was Agrippa himself. He called himself a subtile theologian, skilled lawyer, excellent physician, and marvelous philosopher. To a certain extent he was all of these things and might rightly be called the Renaissance Man of the occult world.

Agrippa was made secretary to the Emperor Maximilian, and earned the title of *chevalier,* which gave him the honorary command of a regiment. Later he became a professor of Hebrew and belles-lettres at the University of Dôle in France.

The one thing that Agrippa really excelled at, however, was irritating people. He has been called "an adept at the gentle art of making enemies." At Dôle he got into an argument with a monk named Catilinet who accused him of heresy, a much more serious charge than mere sorcery, and Agrippa was forced to leave the University.

He went to London where he taught Hebrew for a time and then to Italy where he lectured on alchemy. But Agrippa was unable to keep out of an argument for long. Soon he was embroiled in a furious quarrel with the Italian clergy. Though he remained in Italy for over seven years, passing from one wealthy patron to the next, his status was never secure and life in Italy finally became so uncertain that he was relieved to accept a position as advocate general of the city of Metz, in what is now France.

Naturally he was soon in trouble at Metz. The reasons for his problems in that city were both curious and admirable. Agrippa lived in an age in which a small, apparently laughable point of theology might become the subject of a passionate controversy. At Metz there was a popular belief that St. Anne had three husbands. A minority view held that she had only one husband. Agrippa didn't care much one way or the other, but a friend of his, one J. Faber Stapulensis, strongly supported the single husband view. Agrippa thought he should have a hearing, and ridiculed those who held the saint had three husbands. By this act, Agrippa made some powerful enemies who were just waiting for a chance to get rid of him. They soon got one.

A young peasant girl whose mother had been condemned as a witch was herself arrested for witchcraft. Agrippa honorably and courageously rose to her defense, claiming that such an arrest was irregular because parentage was not sufficient grounds for such a serious accusation. Though he could not prevent the girl from being tortured he did ultimately win her acquittal, and acquittals on the charge of witchcraft were not common. The alleged witch's accusers were even fined for bringing false charges. But the defender of an accused witch, even one who was legally exonerated, always faced the danger of being suspected of the same crime. Agrippa soon found himself charged with sorcery. (Generally sorcery was a less serious charge than witchcraft, though the distinction between the two was not always clear.) Since Agrippa had labored to build the reputation of magician, sorcery was an easy charge to make against him, and he was forced to flee from Metz.

What Agrippa really thought about witchcraft we do not know. But this case indicates that he had not fallen prey to the bloody witch-hunting mania that swept Europe, and particularly his native Germany for over three centuries. One of Agrippa's principal pupils, Johan Weyer, was to become one of the earliest and most outspoken opponents of the witch hunts. Weyer almost certainly picked up some of his humane and rational attitudes from Agrippa himself. A major reason that the Jesuit Del Rio was so intent upon picturing Agrippa as a master sorcerer was that Del Rio himself was a fanatic supporter of witch hunting. He believed that anyone who expressed doubts about the reality of witchcraft must surely be the worst sort of agent of the Devil.

Agrippa, who seemed actively to encourage people to regard him as a master magician, was playing a dangerous game. It gave him power, for people respected and feared him, but it also gave his many enemies a convenient excuse to charge him with any crime.

Agrippa's own attitude toward all the magical arts is enigmatic. Though he enjoyed the reputation of being a great alchemist, in 1526 he wrote to a friend: "Blessed be the Lord, I am a rich man, if there be truth in fable. A man of consideration, long my friend, has brought me seeds of gold and planted them over my furnace within long-necked flasks, putting underneath a little fire as of the sun's heat, and as hens brood over eggs we keep the warmth up night and day, expecting forthwith to produce enormous golden chickens. If all be hatched we shall exceed Midas in wealth, or at least in length of ears . . ."

Was Agrippa ridiculing just this particular alchemical experiment or alchemy in general? We cannot be sure.

After some wandering about Europe, Agrippa wound up as the court physician to Louisa of Savoy, the mother of Francis I of France. As a renowned astrologer as well as physician, he was asked to cast Louisa's horoscope. Accounts differ as to what happened next. According to one story, he refused to cast the horoscope telling the Queen Mother that he would not encourage such idle curiosity. By another account Agrippa had already cast Louisa's horoscope and, convinced that her enemies were going to come out ahead, was unwilling to be the bearer of bad tidings. Louisa would not have taken such news calmly. Whatever Agrippa's reasons, Louisa was furious at him and he was again out of a job. He denounced the Queen Mother as a cruel and perfidious Jezebel. If Agrippa had cast his own horoscope, he might have foreseen that Louisa would ultimately have her revenge.

Agrippa's reputation as a successful wizard was so well established that although sorcery was officially disapproved of by all religious authorities, several monarchs vied for his services. He finally chose to go to the Low Countries under the patronage of Margaret of Austria, who was at that time governess of the land. But there were still powers that stood resolutely against Agrippa, and all those like him. On his way to the Netherlands, Agrippa had to travel through lands controlled by the Duke of Vendôme. The duke refused to give him a pass, saying that he "would sign no passport for a conjurer."

Under Margaret's protection the quarrelsome magician-scholar prospered. He even attained the position of historiographer to the Emperor Charles V, who at the time ruled most of Europe. But after Margaret's death, Agrippa's career went sharply downhill. He returned to France where he was imprisoned because of the things he had once said about Louisa of Savoy, the Queen Mother. At Brussels he was imprisoned again, either on the charge of sorcery or for debt, the records differ.

For a man who had the reputation of being able to turn base metals into gold Agrippa remained remarkably poor all of his life, and he was continually dogged by debts. When he died at Grenoble in 1534 at the age of forty-eight, some say he was poverty-stricken. Again there is a contradictory story indicating that he died amid luxury in the home of a wealthy patron. You may choose whichever version you prefer. For my part, I wish to think he died in luxury, because I like him.

To me Agrippa remains one of the most enigmatic yet attractive characters in occult history. Enigmatic, perhaps only because so many of the details of his life have not survived—and many others have been deliberately falsified by his enemies, his friends, or Agrippa himself. Attractive, because rather than being more superstitious and credulous than his contemporaries he seems to have been more advanced, particularly in his attitude toward witchcraft. Though he wrote several windy treatises on magic and astrology he does not seem to have lost his sense of humor on these subjects.

One of his books, *The Vanity and Nothingness of Human Knowledge,* ridiculed the intellectual and scientific pretensions of the day. Another book, *The Superiority of the Female Sex,* was written to please his favorite patron, Margaret of Austria.

Agrippa's greatest work on occult philosophy was not a book on original theories, but a compilation of the occult ideas of his time and it is quite impossible to determine whether Agrippa subscribed to them or merely collected them. The Inquisition thought this book dangerous enough to try to ban it, and indeed they managed to delay its publication for nearly twenty years. *De occulta philosophia* came out in three volumes, but the part of it that has interested people the most is the fourth volume, the *grimoire,* or magical textbook. This practical magical handbook was and is the most widely read of Agrippa's works, and it's a shame, therefore, that Agrippa never wrote it. The so-called fourth book of occult philosophy was not published until long after the others appeared, and was probably not even written until after Agrippa's death. The real author is unknown. When the *grimoire* was published all who had known Agrippa immediately denounced this fourth book as a fraud—yet it was published, and republished and translated into many languages. So great was Agrippa's reputation as a wizard that a book of spells and potions attributed to him was a sure-fire bestseller in the sixteenth century.

Agrippa's attitude toward magic, as far as it can be pinned down, seems to have been a philosophical rather than a practical one. In a letter written to a friend he says:

"What surprising accounts we meet with, and how great writings there are made of the invincible power of the Magic Art; of the prodigious images of astrologers; of the amazing transmutations of alchemists; and of the blessed Stone by which Midas-like, all metals are transmuted into gold; all of which are found to be vain, fictitious and false, as often as they are practised literally . . . yet such things are delivered and writ by great and grave philosophers, whose traditions who dares to say are false? No, it would be impious to think them lies. There is another meaning than what is written in bare words."

Agrippa continued: "It is an internal spirit within us,

which can very well perform whatsoever the monstrous mathematicians, the prodigious magicians, the wonderful alchemists and the bewitching necromancers can effect."

This is pretty deep philosophy, and not at all what one would expect to hear from the man who had the reputation of being able to call up demons with a few secret words. Nor does it provide much comfort for those who sought and still seek magical miracles.

In the end, it was not Agrippa's works, either genuine or fictitious, that account for his lasting fame, rather it was his flair for publicity and the marvelous stories that have been told about his life.

Paulus Jovius, in his book *Eulogia Doctorum Virorum,* asserted that Agrippa was always attended by a demon in the shape of a large black dog. At the end of his life, so this story goes, Agrippa renounced his magical works. On his death bed he seized the dog and removed its collar, which was covered with magical symbols. "Begone, wretched animal," Agrippa cried, "which has been the cause of my entire destruction." The dog ran away and plunged into the River Saône, and was seen no more.

Agrippa's disciple Weyer was incensed at this particular story. He had lived with Agrippa and had himself often walked this perfectly ordinary black dog on a leash. The stories about the dog started in part because Agrippa was too attached to the animal, and tended to treat it as a member of the family, even allowing it to eat at the table. According to Weyer, Agrippa often did not leave his house for weeks, yet he seemed to be remarkably well informed about what was going on around the town. People began to whisper that it was the demon dog who wandered about to bring his master information.

Agrippa also had a reputation for paying his bills in money that looked perfectly good, but after he departed the scene the coins turned into horn or shell.

Agrippa was supposed to be especially good at calling up spirits to re-enact scenes from history. A story attributed to the Earl of Surrey, and related in a book by Thomas Nash entitled *Adventures of Jack Wilton,* tells the story of how there was a gathering of literary men at the court of the Elector of Saxony. Among those present was Erasmus. Agrippa too was at the court, and hearing of the attendance of the famed wizard the others begged him to give a display of his powers. Erasmus asked to see the ancient Roman orator Cicero deliver one of his celebrated speeches.

"After marshaling the concourse of spectators, Tully [Cicero] appeared at the command of Agrippa, and from the rostrum pronounced the oration, precisely in the words in which it has been handed down to us, with such astonishing animation, so fervent a exaltation of spirit, and such soul-stirring gestures, that all the persons present were ready, like the Romans of old, to pronounce his client innocent of every charge that had been brought against him."

In another story the Earl of Surrey asked Agrippa to show him what his mistress was doing while he was away. "Agrippa accordingly exhibited his magic glass; in which the noble poet [Surrey] saw this beautiful dame, sick, weeping upon her bed, and inconsolable for the absence of her admirer." Surrey was supposed to have made a note of the exact time of this vision, and found afterwards that his mistress actually was weeping for him at the moment he saw the scene in Agrippa's glass.

With his magic glass Agrippa was supposed to have shown King Henry VII hunting at Windsor to Thomas Lord Cromwell, and to amuse the Emperor Charles V he summoned up King David and King Solomon.

How seriously any of these tales were taken at the time is impossible to determine. They were taken seriously enough, however, for some of Agrippa's friends to attempt to defend his reputation against them after his death.

Perhaps Agrippa's friends were not really doing him much of a favor. He seems to have enjoyed the awe and terror inspired by having the reputation of a sorcerer. He doubtless would have been pleased that this reputation followed him beyond the grave, and indeed that it continued to grow for a good many years.

CHAPTER III

John Dee

A POPULAR PICTURE of an occultist might be an ancient man with a flowing beard and a long, loose-fitting robe who sits in his book-lined room lost in the study of ancient and obscure magical manuscripts. In truth most occultists have been more swashbucklers than scholars. But there is at least one who admirably fills this popular stereotype. He was John Dee—I am almost tempted to say the unfortunate John Dee, for though he mislead many people he was surely his own greatest victim.

John Dee, who was of Welsh descent, was born in London on July 13, 1527. His father seems to have held a minor position in the court of Henry VIII, and thus the family was tolerably affluent. Young John showed an early aptitude for scholarship and in 1542 he entered St. John's College, Cambridge. He took his B.A. in 1545 and the next year was elected to a fellowship at his college. Says one of Dee's biographers, he ". . . delighted so much in his books, that he passed regularly eighteen hours every day among them. The other six, he devoted four to sleep and two for refreshment. Such intense application did not injure his health, and could not fail to make him one of the first scholars of his time."

In 1546 when Henry VIII established Trinity College, Dee transferred there. At that time the principal subject he taught was Greek. But like many scholars of his day, Dee was also interested in alchemy, astrology, magic, and other occult practices, and he began to develop a reputation as a magician, or at least a scholar of magic.

At Trinity College he produced a Greek comedy by Aristophanes. In one of the scenes of this play a man carrying a basket of provisions is transported to heaven on the back of a huge beetle. Dee designed the stage effect, and it was so good that "many reports spread abroad of the means how that was effected." The general opinion was that Dee had managed the effect by magic.

Between the years 1547 and 1551 Dee spent most of his time on the Continent, mostly in the Low Countries and in Paris. He did return to England briefly in 1548 to take his M.A., which was the highest degree that he ever received, though he is usually referred to as "Doctor." On the Continent, Dee seems to have studied mostly astronomy and mathematics. In the sixteenth century astronomy often blended easily into astrology, and mathematics into numerology and mysticism. Dee was popular with his academic colleagues, and was once offered a permanent post at the Sorbonne in Paris, but he declined in order to return to England.

Dee's erudition had brought him to the attention of King Edward VI who granted him an annual pension of a hundred crowns. Two years later he became rector of Upton-on-Severn in Worcestershire.

Life appeared to be going along very well for John Dee. He had a comfortable home, an assured income, royal favor, and plenty of time to pursue his studies down whatever bizarre path he chose. But after the short-lived King Edward departed the scene and Bloody Mary came to the throne, Dee was in trouble. Because of some correspondence he had with Princess Elizabeth's household, Dee came under suspicion of plotting against the Queen by magical means. He had apparently been casting favorable horoscopes for Elizabeth, perhaps predicting that she would soon become queen. Dee was arrested and brought before the notorious Star Chamber. He was cleared of the charge of treason, but since his religious views seemed suspiciously heretical he was confined to the Bishop of London's prison until 1555. He was released only after he promised to behave himself.

When Queen Elizabeth ascended the throne in 1558, Dee's fortunes really began to rise. He had already been a favorite of Elizabeth's before she became queen and he was asked to calculate astrologically a favorable day for her coronation.

Elizabeth made some rather elaborate promises about what she was going to do for Dee, but most of these promises were never kept. Making unfulfillable promises to those she thought could help her was one of the Queen's trademarks. Still Dee did quite well for himself as the Queen's unofficial magician-in-chief. He bought a fine home by the river at Mortlake and amassed a large collection of what has been described as "curious books and manuscripts."

As a scholar Dee performed some real services. Pope Gregory XIII reformed the calendar in 1582, and Dee was brought in to make the necessary calculations to bring the new Gregorian calendar into agreement with the English calendar. His work was in vain, however, for the conservative Anglican bishops refused to go along with any change, and England remained out of step with the rest of Europe for another hundred and seventy years. Dee also promoted a national library, a coast guard, and telescopes for army officers.

But it was magic in one form or another which intrigued Dee more and more, and became the basis for his continued favor at court. The Queen heard of Dee's celebrated crystal ball and traveled to his home at Mortlake to see it. But when she discovered that Dee's wife had recently died in the house she refused to enter, so the crystal was brought out for her inspection.

When a comet appeared in the skies Dee was summoned by the Queen to explain its significance. On another occasion he was called in when a waxen image of the Queen was found in Lincoln's Inn Field with a pin stuck in it. Dee's job was to make sure magically that this evil charm did not harm Her Majesty. Whatever he did must have worked, for Elizabeth lived on for another quarter of a century and became one of England's greatest monarchs.

For the most part, however, Dee stayed in his library, where, bent over his books, he explored the Talmudic mysteries, the Rosicrucian theories, and a host of other obscure and occult subjects. What happened next is described by Charles Mackay, a sharp critic of magic: "By dint of continually brooding upon the subject his imagination became so diseased, that he at last persuaded himself that an angel appeared to him, and promised to be his friend and companion as long as he lived."

Dee's diary records the progression of his mystic experiences. He first saw spirits in his crystal globe on May 25, 1581. In November 1582 he was praying when suddenly he saw a dazzling light in the west window of his room. In the midst of the light he perceived the great angel Uriel. Dee was struck dumb, but the angel smiled at him, and presented him with a new and more wondrous crystal. Uriel told Dee that whenever he wanted to converse with the spirits or angels he only had to gaze into the crystal, and the mysteries of the future would be unveiled to him. (This crystal, or at least a crystal from Dee's collection, is now in the British Museum. It is a polished globe of smoky quartz. Another of Dee's crystals is supposed to have been a polished lump of coal.)

At this point of his life John Dee was described as a tall, slender man with a sallow complexion and a long white beard. He customarily wore a long loose-fitting gown with hanging sleeves. He was known to be kind and friendly, though many people, particularly children, avoided him because of his reputation for being a wizard. He was the perfect picture of a scholarly occultist, deluded perhaps, but honest. That was to change.

The problem with Uriel's marvelous crystal was that it did not work like a television set. One simply did not turn it on and gaze into it to see the future. Dee had to work himself into a state of mystic exaltation in order to see anything. Unfortunately, when this state of exaltation passed Dee could remember nothing of what he had seen or heard—a thoroughly unsatisfactory situation. So Dee decided to employ a skryer, an adept at the art of crystal gazing. The skryer would look into the crystal and describe what he saw while Dee would write it down. The first skryer must have been an honest man because he didn't see anything in the crystal. Then the villain of this piece, Edward Kelly, appeared on the scene.

By virtually everybody's reckoning—occultists and non-occultists alike—Kelly was a rogue. Edward Kelly or Kelley (or Talbot, which seems to have been an alias) was born in 1555. For a time he was apprenticed to an apothecary. He was also briefly a student at Oxford, but never earned a degree.

He popped up in London, where he got the reputation of being a crooked lawyer. At Lancaster in about 1580 he was convicted of forgery, was put in the pillory and had his ears cut off. Later he always wore a hat which covered the sides of his head and disguised his earlessness. Also at Lancaster he seems to have gotten into some trouble for digging up a corpse for the purpose of necromancy—that is, questioning the dead about the future.

A seventeenth-century book, *Ancient Funerall Monuments* by John Weever, describes the supposed necromantic adventures of Kelly:

"This diabolical questioning of the dead for the knowledge of future accidents was put into practice by the said Kelley, who upon a certain night in the park of Walton-le-Dale in the county of Lancaster with one Paul Waring (his fellow companion in such deeds of darkness) invoked some of the Infernal Regiment to know certain passages in the life, as also what might be known by the Devil's foresight of the manner of time of the death of a noble young gentleman, as then in wardship. The black ceremonies of the night being ended, Kelley demanded of one of the gentleman's servants what corpse was the last buried in Law churchyard, a church thereunto adjoining, who told him of a poor man that was buried there but the same day. He and the said Waring entreated this foresaid servant to go with them to the grave of the man so lately interred, which he did; and withal did help them to dig up the carcase of the poor caitiff, whom by their incantations they made him (or rather some evil spirit through his organs) to speak, who delivered strange predictions concerning the said gentleman. I was told this by the said serving man a secondary actor in that dismal abhorred business . . ."

In March 1582 Edward Kelly appeared at Mortlake to seek

an audience with the celebrated Dr. Dee. Kelly wore a "black skullcap, which fitting close to his head, and descending over both his cheeks, not only concealed his loss [of ears], but gave him a very solemn and oracular appearance." As a matter of fact, it seems that Dee never actually knew of his assistant's earlessness, though they worked closely together for years.

Kelly said that he was a humble student of the occult, and had hoped for some instructions at the feet of the great Dr. Dee. Dee was careful at first, but soon enough Kelly had talked him into producing his wondrous crystal. After the proper prayers and incantations, Kelly offered to serve as skryer.

His success was immediate and spectacular. According to Kelly the angel Uriel appeared to him. He gave directions for the invocation of other spirits, and ordered that an evil spirit named Lundrumguffa, who was particularly dangerous to Dee, should be dismissed.

Uriel also stressed that Dee should hire Kelly as his regular skryer, and that the two of them should always work together. Remember now that Dee saw none of this. He simply sat down in a corner and recorded what Kelly told him. But since he had often conversed with the spirits himself, he was convinced that Kelly was doing the same, and that every word Kelly repeated to him was in the nature of a revelation from the world of the spirits. Kelly was hired as regular skryer at an annual salary of fifty pounds, but he got frequent raises by threatening to quit. Indeed, he quarreled loudly and incessantly with his employer but was ultimately always able to bend the scholar to his will. There is a theory that Kelly was sent to spy on Dee, but it seems far more likely that he was a simple opportunist.

Dee's renown at this time was formidable. People flocked

to Mortlake to have their horoscopes cast by the great astrologer, and his fees were appropriately high. But much of his money he sank into building his great library and into his alchemical experiments. Adds one historian of alchemy, "No doubt much of Dee's gold was transmuted into a lining for Kelly's pockets."

In July of 1583 the Earl of Leicester brought a Polish nobleman named Albert Laski to see Dee and Kelly. Though Laski lived in the grand manner of an extremely wealthy man, his fortune had really been dwindling away at an alarming rate. Like so many other men, Count Laski hoped to restore his wealth through the wizardry of alchemy. Scholars differ as to whether what followed was solely the invention of Kelly, or whether Dee himself cooperated in the deception.

Lewis Spence, who is generally sympathetic to Dee, has written: "On a careful perusal of Dee's diary it is impossible to come to any other conclusion than that he was imposed upon by Kelly, and accepted his revelations as the actual utterances of the spirits; and it seems probable that the clever, plastic, slippery Kelly not only knew something of the optical delusions then practised by the pretended necromancers, but possessed considerable ventriloquial powers which largely assisted in his nefarious deceptions."

Laski became a regular visitor at Mortlake, and engaged with Dee and Kelly in what can only be described as spiritualist seances. Writes Dee: "Suddenly there seemed to come out of the oratory a spiritual creature, like a pretty girl of seven or nine years of age, attired on her head, with her hair rolled up before and hanging down behind, with a gown of silk, of changeable red and green, and with a train. She seemed to play up and down, and seemed to go in and out behind the books; and as she seemed to go between them the books displaced themselves, and made way for her."

This spiritual creature turned out to be named Madimi. Dee never claimed he had actually seen Madimi or heard her. Everything he recorded was told to him by Kelly. But in the scene described above he appears to indicate that he actually saw or believed that he saw books being moved about as the spiritual creature passed among them.

With the aid of Madimi and other spirits Kelly and Dee outlined a fantastic future for Count Laski. He was, first of all, to possess the Philosophers' Stone, the goal of all alchemical research. With it the Count would become wealthy beyond his wildest dreams, for the Stone had the power to turn base metals into gold. The fabled Philosophers' Stone was also said to be the key to eternal or at least very long life, so Laski would live for centuries as well. Not only that, he was to become King of Poland, and a famous general who would win many battles over the Saracens, which would make his name honored throughout all Christendom.

Moreover, the spirits practically made an Englishman out of the Polish count by tracing his ancestry back to "Roderick the Great Prince of Wales."

How much of this extravagant nonsense Laski actually swallowed is impossible to know. But he must have swallowed quite a bit for he returned to Mortlake again and again to hear more, and he helped to finance Dee in his expensive alchemical experiments.

Though Dee had remained in the Queen's good graces there were ominous clouds on the horizon. The clergy was thundering against magical activities in England. Preaching before the Queen herself, Bishop Jessel observed: "It may please your grace to understand that witches and sorcerers within these last few years are marvellously increased within your grace's realm. Your grace's subjects pine away even unto death, their color fadeth, their flesh rotteth, their senses become bereft. I pray God they never practise further upon the subject."

The prospect of being trapped in the middle of a witch hunt that seemed to be building up was not a comfortable one for John Dee and Edward Kelly. An extended trip abroad at this time seemed wise. And who better to pay for the trip than the alchemically obsessed Albert Laski.

Despite his damaged fortunes Laski always maintained an appearance of great opulence, and in their travels Dee and Kelly imitated their new patron at his expense. Dee and Kelly took their wives (Dee had remarried a much younger woman), servants, and an enormous amount of baggage, and proceeded slowly and luxuriously to Laski's estates near Cracow. Shortly after the party left England a mob invaded Dee's house at Mortlake and destroyed much of his valuable library, and many of the magical objects with which he had surrounded himself.

For five months Dee, Kelly, and company remained at Cracow, and engaged in the very expensive business of alchemy. Time and again Laski was forced to borrow money in order to buy supplies for the experiments. He was always led on by the belief or hope that very soon he would have all the gold he desired.

Whether Laski's patience or funds ran out first we do not know. But in July of 1584 he decided he had to get rid of his expensive guests. He sent them packing but gave them letters of introduction to the Emperor Rudolf II at Prague. The Emperor's interest in alchemy was well known, and he had sponsored many alchemists. But after a single interview with

Dee and Kelly he seems to have been unimpressed, and their pleas were ignored. Meanwhile the Papal Nuncio complained to the Emperor about harboring the heretical magicians, and Dee and Kelly found it wise to depart from Prague in a hurry.

King Stephen of Poland was their next hope, but after a single seance the King declared the whole business to be fraudulent.

The magicians were now badly in need of a patron but organized hostility to them had grown, and for a time they were forced to support themselves as common fortune-tellers. They even circulated the rumor that they actually possessed the Philosophers' Stone, which they had dug up at Glastonbury Abbey before leaving England. This ancient abbey has long had supernatural associations. The Stone was supposed to have been prepared by no less a personage than St. Dunstan himself.

Dee and Kelly began to look longingly toward England again, and they sent Queen Elizabeth a most unusual gift, a brass warming pan with a gold disk in it. Dee explained that Kelly had turned the brass cutout into gold.

Elizabeth was pleased with the gift, but not pleased enough to invite the pair to come back to England, so it was fortunate that another patron appeared on the Continent. He was Count Rosenberg, a wealthy Bohemian nobleman with large estates at Trebona. The Count had plenty of gold; he desired power. Soon the spirits through the agency of Kelly informed him that he would become the King of Poland, that he would live five hundred years, and so forth. In return Count Rosenberg financed alchemical experiments as well as supporting Dee and Kelly in luxury.

At about this time Kelly got a surprising order from the spirits—the spirits had decided that he and Dee should share wives. Perhaps the order was not so surprising after all. Kelly had always hated his own wife and been attracted to Dee's. The women were quite horrified, and even Dee who had gone along with Kelly on practically everything objected to this suggestion. Perhaps the spirits had spoken figuratively, he said. But Kelly insisted, and ranted and raved about how dangerous it would be to ignore a command of the spirits. So Dee agreed and in his diary he duly recorded:

"On Sunday, the third day of May, Anno 1587, I, John Dee, Edward Kelley, and our two wives, covenanted with God and subscribed the same for indissoluble and inviolable unities, charity, and friendship keeping between us four; and all things between us to be common, as God by sundry means willed us to do."

This new arrangement increased discord in the already none-too-harmonious household. Kelly threatened to leave more loudly than ever and Dee began looking around for a new skryer. He chose his eight-year-old son, Arthur. But when the boy gazed into the crystal no spirits appeared, and Dee was forced once again to call upon Kelly.

But the stormy partnership lasted only a few more months. Kelly took his reputed Philosophers' Stone and departed for Prague, once again to try his luck with the Emperor Rudolf. But the Emperor was still unimpressed, and this time had Kelly thrown in jail for wizardry and sorcery. There Kelly languished for several months, until, with the aid of a friendly letter from Queen Elizabeth, he was released. Kelly wandered about Europe for a few years, telling fortunes here and pretending to make gold there, but it was a hard life.

Finally he was again thrown into prison, and this time the very serious charge of heresy was added to the charge of sorcery. It looked as though Edward Kelly was going to spend the rest of his life in prison. According to one account his end came this way:

"He twisted his bed-clothes into a rope, one stormy night in February 1595, and let himself down from the window of his dungeon, situated at the top of a very high tower. Being a corpulent man, the rope gave way, and he was precipitated to the ground. He broke two of his ribs and both his legs and was otherwise so much injured, that he expired a few days afterwards."

Dee quit the continent for England, where he still retained a measure of the Queen's favor. He apparently arrived in England with a huge baggage train and protected by a guard of twenty soldiers, though where he could have gotten the money for such an entourage is hard to imagine unless Count Rosenberg had supplied a liberal parting gift.

But Dee was certainly in need of money when he arrived. The Queen received him at Richmond and awarded him a pension of two hundred pounds a year. But the great days were clearly over. One highly sympathetic biographer notes:

"Here ends the prosperity and greatness of this extraordinary man. If he possessed the power of turning all baser metals into gold he certainly acted unadvisedly in surrendering this power to his confederate immediately before his return to his native country. He parted at the same time with his gift of prophecy since, though he brought away with him his miraculous stone, and at one time appointed one Bartholomew and another one Hickman, his interpreters to look into the stone, to see the marvelous sights it was expected to disclose, and to hear the voices and report the words that issued from it, the experiments proved in both instances abortive."

Still some people believed that John Dee was a magician.

The year after his return to England he was writing to defend himself against the charge of sorcery.

From all indications the Queen had now entirely lost whatever faith she once might have had in Dee. He bombarded her with letters, pleading for money, but her response was not generous. Around 1595 he obtained the position of warden of the college at Manchester but he was never happy there. In 1602 or 1603, when his health began to fail, he gave up the post and returned to Mortlake.

Dee's old patron Queen Elizabeth died in 1603, and her successor, James, had scant sympathy for the aging scholar of magic. Besides, King James was a renowned cheap skate. Dee wrote the new King appeal after appeal, claiming that he was forced to sell some of his books in order to obtain a meal. Nothing worked. Dee cast horoscopes and otherwise supported himself as a common fortune-teller until 1608, when he died at the age of eighty-one. He was buried at Mortlake.

His son, Arthur, who had failed so miserably at crystal gazing went on to become alchemist and physician to the Tsar of Russia and later physician to Charles I of England.

Dee's sessions with Kelly appear to be obvious precursors of modern spiritualism. But as a matter of fact, they never seemed to lead to anything. After Dee's death most interest centered upon his supposed success with alchemy, rather than with anything the spirits might have to say.

It was well over a century before talking with spirits became widely popular.

CHAPTER IV

St. Germain

"He is called an Italian, a Spaniard, a Pole, a somebody who married a great fortune in Mexico and ran away with her jewels to Constantinople, a priest, a fiddler, a vast nobleman."

So wrote Horace Walpole of that most mysterious of all occult adventurers, the Comte de St. Germain. And Walpole expressed only the more moderate views of the enigmatic Count's background. Wrote Charles Mackay: "Some believed, from the Jewish cast of his handsome countenance, that he was the 'wandering Jew'; others asserted that he was the issue of an Arabian princess, and that his father was a salamander; while others, more reasonable, affirmed him to be the son of a Portuguese Jew established at Bourdeaux."

Most of those who have attempted to trace St. Germain's tangled and obscure history tend to believe that he was indeed a Portuguese Jew born around the year 1710, though there is certainly no hard evidence to back up this belief. His real name and place of birth are unknown.

The earliest mention of St. Germain places him in Germany, where he apparently was selling a fluid he claimed was the elixir of eternal youth. This sort of obvious fraud seems rather crude for the elegant St. Germain. In any event, either the elixir or more probably the charm of St. Germain so captivated the Maréchal de Belle-Isle that he induced St. Germain to settle in Paris. Though St. Germain spoke at least half a dozen languages, and was an intimate in courts and wealthy homes throughout Europe, the bulk of his time seems to have been spent in France, and it is in France that he attained his greatest fame and influence.

To understand St. Germain's popularity it is necessary to say a few words about the world in which he flourished. The eighteenth century has been called the Age of Reason. It was also a golden age for science. In England, Sir Isaac Newton was literally transforming mankind's view of the universe. In France the primary figure of the eighteenth century was the skeptical Voltaire. Anticlericalism was rampant, all the old ideas of religion, of the nature of man, of reality itself were under skeptical scrutiny. Yet occultism flourished. It has been said that the eighteenth century was skeptical of everything but occultism and in this respect it has many parallels with the second half of the twentieth century. But there were differences. A principal one, as far as claims to occult powers were concerned, was that in the eighteenth century belief in alchemy still held on though it was losing its popularity. St. Germain's younger contemporary Cagliostro was really the last great claimant to alchemical powers in Europe. In St. Germain's day, however, many still believed that a method for turning base metals into gold would be found, and had perhaps already been found and secretly used by certain adepts.

Belief was also strong that through alchemical methods the

adept could produce an elixir of life which conferred either extremely long life or immortality.

St. Germain himself did not fritter away his life bending over furnaces and retorts like an ordinary alchemical puffer. Nor did he dress in the flowing robes of a sorcerer. He appeared always as an elegant gentleman, but many believed that he had discovered the secret of boundless wealth, and the secret of immortality. It was commonly said that St. Germain was immortal and had already lived hundreds of years. While the Count never actively spread such stories, he never exactly denied them either. Occasionally he did relax a bit and ridicule the foolishness of those who believed in his immortality.

In the *Memoirs of Madame du Hausset,* who served in the suite of the King's mistress, Madame de Pompadour, there are some revealing stories concerning St. Germain. St. Germain was an undoubted charmer, and he soon was allowed entrée to Pompadour's dressing room, a favor granted to very few. While he would often lead Pompadour on to believing he was several hundred years old, he could also be a good deal more frank when he desired.

Writes Madame du Hausset:

"One day, Madame said to him, in my presence, 'What was the personal appearance of Francis I? He was a king I should have liked.' 'He was, indeed, very captivating,' replied St. Germain; and he proceeded to describe his face and person, as that of a man whom he had accurately observed. 'It is a pity he was too ardent. I could have given him some good advice, which would have saved him from all his misfortunes but he would not have followed it; for it seems as if a fatality attended princes forcing them to shut their eyes to the wisest counsel.' 'Was his court very brilliant?' inquired Madame de

Pompadour. 'Very,' replied the count; 'but those of his grandsons surpassed it. In the time of Mary Stuart and Margaret of Valois, it was a land of enchantment—a temple sacred to pleasures of every kind.' Madame said, laughing, 'You seem to have seen all this.' 'I have an excellent memory,' said he, 'and have read the history of France with great care. I sometimes amuse myself, not by making but by letting it be believed that I lived in olden times.'

" 'But you do not tell us your age,' said Madame de Pompadour to him on another occasion; 'and yet you pretend you are very old. The Countess de Gergy, who was, I believe, ambassadress at Vienna some fifty years ago, says she saw you there exactly the same as you now appear.'

" 'It is true, Madame,' replied St. Germain; 'I knew Madame de Gergy many years ago.'

" 'But according to her account, you must be more than a hundred years old?'

" 'That is not impossible,' said he, laughing; 'but it is much more possible that the good lady is in her dotage.'

" 'You gave her an elixir, surprising for the effects it produced; for she says, that during a length of time she only appeared to be eighty-four, the age at which she took it. Why don't you give it to the king?'

" 'Oh, madame,' he exclaimed, 'the physicians would have me broken on the wheel, were I to think of drugging his majesty.' "

Madame du Hausset says that at the time she knew St. Germain he appeared to be about fifty years old, of average size, but with a fine, expressive face.

When people pressed St. Germain for the secret elixir of life, he would often reply by saying that moderation in all things was far superior to any elixir in attaining longevity.

But he never actually denied that there was such an elixir, and people persisted in believing that he did indeed possess the magical fluid but was intent upon keeping it a secret. As St. Germain had told Madame de Pompadour, he did not make people believe absurd things about him, but he let them believe such things, by acting enigmatic and never affirming or denying anything.

There is a story that at one point a group of young men tried to mock St. Germain by ridiculing his supposed longevity. One of them dressed up as St. Germain and attended parties at several houses where the Count himself was not personally known. Of course everybody in Paris had heard of St. Germain, and those who had never met him were eager to listen to the stories of this false St. Germain.

The impostor spoke of Jesus as a close friend. He said that he had often warned Jesus to be less romantic and rash, or he would finish his career miserably.

St. Germain himself would never have made such a statement, it was simply too outrageous, and besides it was a blasphemy which might have landed him in serious trouble. But when no trouble seemed forthcoming, he never did go to any great pains to deny these stories either.

With good friends St. Germain rarely pretended to an age of more than about three hundred years. He would speak of long-dead kings and heroes in such detail that many were led to believe that he had actually been on the scene. However, he was usually careful not to commit himself fully on this point.

With a more credulous audience he might indicate he had lived much longer. Perhaps the most celebrated of all the stories about St. Germain concerns a dinner party at which he was speaking with easy familiarity of King Richard the Lion-

Hearted, and of some of the conversations they had while in Palestine during the Crusades. When some of the guests looked astonished and skeptical, St. Germain turned to his valet, who was standing behind his chair, and asked him to confirm the truth of the story.

"I really cannot say, sir," the servant replied, with perfect coolness; "you forget, sir, I have only been five hundred years in your service!"

"Ah! true," said St. Germain. "I remember now—it was a little before your time!"

"These fools of Parisians," St. Germain was once supposed to have confided to the Baron de Gleichen, "believe me to be more than five hundred years old; and since they will have it so, I confirm them in their idea. Not but that I really am much older than I appear."

Next to his reputation for longevity, the Comte de St. Germain attracted attention because of his reputation for being fabulously wealthy. He generally dressed rather simply, though in excellent taste, and he lived mainly on the hospitality of his aristocratic friends. Yet St. Germain does seem to have possessed a considerable fortune in precious stones, some of which he wore on the buckles of his shoes.

Again to quote Madame du Hausset:

"The count came to see Madame de Pompadour, who was very ill, and lay on the sofa. He showed her diamonds enough to furnish a king's treasury. Madame sent for me to see all those beautiful things. I looked at them with an air of utmost astonishment; but I made signs to her that I thought them all false. The count felt for something in a pocket book about twice as large as a spectacle-case, and at length drew out two or three little paper packets, which he unfolded, and exhibited a superb ruby. He threw on the table, with a contemptuous air, a little cross of green and white stones. I looked at it, and said it was not to be despised. I then put it on, and admired it greatly. The Count begged me to accept it; I refused. He urged me to take it. At length he pressed so warmly, that madame, seeing it could not be worth more than a thousand livres, made me a sign to accept it. I took the cross, much pleased with the Count's politeness."

Thus in order to simulate great wealth St. Germain seems to have mixed genuine jewels in with a great number of false ones—and then made an elaborate show of disdaining all wealth. Naturally around so mysterious and alluring a character, the tales of his riches grew with each retelling. Many thought that the source of St. Germain's wealth was possession of the secret of turning base metals into gold, though St. Germain usually displayed wealth in precious stones rather than gold. Others believed that he was a member of the secret order of the Rosicrucians, who were rumored to possess the secret of drawing precious stones out of the earth.

In fact, St. Germain does seem to have been a moderately rich man, and the source of his income is genuinely mysterious. Some suspect that he made a good deal of money selling his elixir of life, but there are even stronger suspicions that he was a paid spy. Horace Walpole wrote that in 1743 St. Germain was actually arrested in London for being a spy. And in 1758 Voltaire wrote a letter to the King of Prussia in which he stated that St. Germain was definitely in the pay of foreign governments.

In the eighteenth century the image of a spy was quite different than it is today. It was common even for very high officials of one government to be in the pay of another. The spy's business was not so much to steal state secrets, but rather to report on the mood, the intentions, and even the gossip of the court. Since practically everybody engaged in spying, St. Germain could easily have been a spy, and made a good living from it, though he was never really intimate with the centers of power in France, and it is hard to see how he could have provided much useful information.

One final unanswered question about St. Germain's enigmatic life: Was he really a member of some secret mystic society? Secret societies like the Rosicrucians were very popular in eighteenth-century France. With his love of theatrical mystification, St. Germain may well have been a member of one or perhaps several secret societies.

He has the reputation of being the Grand Master of some powerful but super-secret occult brotherhood. This reputation comes not so much from anything St. Germain himself said but rather from an account set down by his admirer and imitator Giuseppe Balsamo, better known under his assumed title of Alessandro, Comte de Cagliostro, or simply Cagliostro.

Cagliostro attributed much of his reputed occult knowledge to a meeting with St. Germain, which he said changed the course of his entire life. There are several versions of this celebrated meeting, none of them very trustworthy, for they came either from Cagliostro himself, and he was a noted liar, or from his bitter enemies, who were no more truthful. But for lack of any other source of information, here is how it went.

St. Germain told Cagliostro and his wife to meet him at two in the morning. As ordered, the pair came to St. Germain's Temple of Mystery wearing white robes bound by red girdles. The drawbridge was lowered, and a very tall man wearing a gray robe led the pair across it and into a dimly lighted chamber. Suddenly folding doors sprang open, revealing a room illuminated by hundreds of wax candles. St. Germain sat upon an altar, and at his feet two acolytes swung golden censers, which filled the air with aromatic perfumes.

According to a book called *Lives of the Alchemystical Philosophers,* the interview proceeded thus: "The divinity [St. Germain in costume] bore upon his breast a diamond pentagram of almost intolerable radiance. A majestic statue, white and diaphanous, upheld on the steps of the altar a vase inscribed 'Elixir of Immortality,' while a vast mirror was on the wall, and before it a living being, majestic as the statue, walked to and fro. Above the mirror were these singular words—'Store House of Wandering Souls.' The most solemn silence prevailed in this sacred retreat, but at length a voice, which seemed hardly a voice, pronounced these words—'Who are you? Whence come you? What would you?' Then the Count and Countess Cagliostro prostrated themselves, and the former answered after a long pause, 'I come to invoke the God of the faithful, the Son of Nature, the Sire of Truth. I come to demand of him one of the fourteen thousand seven hundred secrets which are treasured in his breast. I come to proclaim myself his slave, his apostle, his martyr.' "

The Count and Countess then undergo various trials, typical of initiation into a secret society. At one point a draped figure tells them: "Know ye that the *arcanum* of our great art is the government of mankind, and that the one means to rule them is never to tell them the truth. Do not foolishly regulate your actions according to the rules of common sense; rather outrage reason and courageously maintain every unbelievable absurdity. Remember . . . that it is a mania with mortals to be immortal, to know the future without understanding the present, and to be spiritual while all that surrounds them is material."

After a long speech in which St. Germain denounces everyone else in the world as a pack of idiots and knaves, this curious initiation ends with a great feast.

"During the course of the banquet the two guests were informed that the Elixir of Immortality was merely Tokay [wine] coloured green or red according to the necessities of the case. Several essential precepts were enjoined upon them, among others that they must detest, avoid, and calumniate men of understanding, but flatter, foster, and blind fools, that they must spread abroad with much mystery the intelligence that the Comte de St. Germain was five hundred years old, and that they must make gold, but dupes before all."

The original source of this strange account of Cagliostro's interview with St. Germain is unknown. Cagliostro always credited St. Germain with having a great influence on his life, and incidentally with being the founder of Freemasonry. The numerous enemies of Freemasonry were always constructing imaginary accounts of what went on during Masonic initiations, and this meeting of St. Germain and Cagliostro sounds like one of these imaginary accounts. Still, while the events described may never have taken place at all, the worldly cynicism expressed by St. Germain in this interview may not have been too wide of the mark.

Around the year 1760 St. Germain left Paris, for political reasons it was rumored. He may have gone to London for a while and to St. Petersburg, but we can't be sure. Ultimately, he appeared at the court of the Prince of Hesse-Cassel, in Germany. Here it seems he lived well under the patronage of his friend the Prince until his death around the year 1782.

St. Germain's reputation as an immortal occult master followed him beyond the grave. From time to time he has been listed by various occult groups as a member of a distant order of "masters," "adepts," or "illuminati," who through their knowledge of occult science have found the secret of immortality, and from some distant place manage to control worldly events, and pass their knowledge on to carefully chosen disciples.

Perhaps the weirdest of all the incarnations of St. Germain was when he was made the patron saint of the I AM movement, which existed in the United States in the 1920s and 1930s. The I AM movement was half occultism, half American fascism. The group had a storm trooper corps named the Minute Men of St. Germain. St. Germain himself was pictured as a bearded white-robed character, which the elegant eighteenth-century adventurer resembled not at all.

The founders of the I AM movement were a couple of promoters named Guy and Edna Ballard. Ballard claimed he had gotten his idea for the movement after meeting St. Germain on Mt. Shasta. The Ballards kept threatening to kill President Franklin Roosevelt, whom they detested, with "Saint Germain's Blue Ray," and to take over the government so that they could replace the red in the American flag—since red was the color of Communism—with gold, a more American color.

This foolish cult limped on into the early forties, but by that time America was at war with Germany, and groups sympathetic to fascism were less popular than ever.

The final irony is that by choosing St. Germain as the spiritual father of their movement, the violently anti-Semitic Ballards may have chosen a Jew.

CHAPTER V

Emanuel Swedenborg

AT THE AGE OF fifty-six after leading a useful, successful, but exceedingly uninteresting life, Emanuel Swedenborg went quietly, pleasantly, but most decidedly mad. Swedenborg's followers and admirers, and there are still many today, would hotly dispute that particular judgment, and insist that he had received a revelation from God. Whatever the case, Swedenborg's life changed radically, and that change profoundly influenced the trend of occult thinking down to the present day. Swedenborg is the most illustrious and respectable of all the occult visionaries.

Emanuel Swedenborg was born Emanuel Swedberg in 1688 in Stockholm, Sweden. He was the son of a Lutheran bishop and a teacher of theology, albeit the bishop was a bit on the unorthodox side and his ideas were denounced by many of his fellow clergymen. Young Emanuel was, without question, brilliant. He was graduated as a geologist from the University of Uppsala at the age of twenty-one and spent the next several years pursuing studies in the natural sciences in many parts of Europe. By the time he returned to Stockholm he was, among other things, an accomplished engineer. In 1716 he was appointed by Charles XII to the Royal College of Mines, a position he retained until his entire life changed. His contributions to Swedish society were considered so great that the family was ennobled in 1719 by Queen Ulrica Eleanora. It was at this point that the family name was changed to Swedenborg.

During this first period of his life, Swedenborg was enormously versatile and energetic. He became a member of the Swedish Diet, and was considered an expert on economics as well as science, and thus was a figure of considerable political influence.

Privately Swedenborg continued his natural science investigations and speculations. In the weighty books that he wrote on the origins of things he anticipated many ideas which were later to be scientifically proven. Say his admirers, these were "prophetic anticipations." Say his detractors, they were lucky hits that are inevitable in a barrage of wild speculation. Swedenborg was also a prolific inventor. During this period of his life he was rightly considered one of the most knowledgeable men in Europe.

Swedenborg seemed to possess none of the personal eccentricities that make most occultists so fascinating to read about and irritating to know. Even after his "illumination" Swedenborg was reported as being unfailingly pleasant, courteous, and bland. He seems to have been basically a rather shy individual who talked with a pronounced stutter, yet he was certainly no recluse. He moved with ease in the wealthiest and most aristocratic circles in many of the countries of Europe.

When Swedenborg was young he had apparently been turned down by two different young ladies whom he had asked to marry him, and as a result he never married. However, up until the time of his "illumination," when he adopted an ascetic mode of life, he did occasionally talk of getting married and settling down.

Through the first fifty-six years of his life Swedenborg wrote no specifically religious works, though he had certainly not become an unbeliever. In the last scientific book he wrote, *The Animal Kingdom,* a study of the anatomy of animals, he also attempted to prove the existence of the soul. But such speculation was not at all unusual for scientific men of his day.

All in all, there was nothing in the first two thirds of his life to foreshadow in any way what was to happen during the final third. This change, or "illumination" as Swedenborg called it, was brought about by a series of dreams or visions. It seems to have taken place very rapidly, almost overnight. The first "illumination" Swedenborg recorded took place at Easter 1744. From that time on he believed that he had been chosen to see the spirit world, converse with the dead, and reveal the new truths that he learned to all of mankind. He was, he said, the sole intermediary between this world and the next, and he was the new prophet who would reveal the true spiritual meaning of the gospels.

At an earlier time such a claim would doubtless have earned Swedenborg a heretic's death at the stake. Today the same claim might easily prove a one-way ticket to a mental institution. In the tolerant and enlightened eighteenth century, Swedenborg was allowed to have his say. Though many of Swedenborg's friends thought that he had indeed gone mad, they found him to be the same courteous and earnest fellow that he had been before his "illumination." The only observable difference in his behavior—aside from telling people how he had just spoken with Plato or some other long-dead luminary—was that he spent an increasingly large part of his life in a trance. These trances might last as long as three days, and occasionally his friends and neighbors were not sure whether he was dead or alive. But in fact the long trances and rigidly ascetic life did not seem to affect his health at all. He remained in excellent health and was quite active until the end of his very long life. He did not even complete his major book on religion until he was eighty-two.

There were to be no deathbed confessions for Emanuel Swedenborg. During his final illness he allowed a Swedish minister to visit him, though he had not attended regular church services in many years. Swedenborg greeted the minister and said with great seriousness: "As truly as you see me before your eyes, so true is everything that I have written; and I could have said more had it been permitted. When you enter eternity you will see everything, and then you and I shall have much to talk about."

Swedenborg differs from many other mystics of history by the natural, almost commonplace way in which he accepted his trances and visions. Occasionally his mystic experiences were of an ecstatic nature. Of one he wrote: "I had in my mind and body the feeling of an indescribable delight, so that had it been in any higher degree the whole body would have been, as it were, dissolved in pure joy. In a word, I was in heaven and heard speech which no human tongue can utter, with the life that there is there, with the glory and inmost delight that flow from it."

Most of the time, however, Swedenborg slipped in and out of trances as easily as you or I might change our socks. Sometimes trances came upon him involuntarily, but he claimed to be able to put himself into a trance by controlling his breathing. But he did not have to be in a trance to see the spirits. Occasionally in the middle of an ordinary conversation he would turn aside to chat with spirits whom he perceived to be nearby.

No wonder many of his friends believed that he had gone insane. This view probably protected him from being ostracized as a religious eccentric, for his views were unorthodox in the extreme. People also seemed reassured by the entirely casual way in which Swedenborg treated the wonders that he said he was witnessing.

John Christian Cuneo, an Amsterdam merchant and friend of Swedenborg's, recorded this event in his journal: "I visited him [Swedenborg] last Thursday and found him writing as usual. He told me that the same morning he had talked for three hours in the spirit kingdom with the deceased King of Sweden. He had already met him there on Wednesday, thus the day before, but when he saw the King was engaged in a deep conversation with the Queen, who is still living, he did not wish to disturb him."

Cuneo, who was used to the fact that this friend habitually conversed with the dead, expressed surprise only that the dead King was able to talk to Queen Louisa Ulrica, who was still alive. Swedenborg calmly assured the merchant that this was perfectly natural because, "Every man has his good or evil angel who is constantly with him, but sometimes withdraws from him and appears in the spirit kingdom. Of this the living man knows nothing but the spirit everything. Such an associate spirit has everything in complete conformity with his human companion. In the spirit kingdom he has visibly the same figure, the same form of countenance, and the same tone of voice, as the man on earth; he also wears the same clothes. In a word this associate spirit of the Queen appears no other wise than as the Queen herself, as he has so often seen her in Stockholm . . ."

Another characteristic of Swedenborg that doubtless saved him from any persecution by society was that he never attempted to form his own church or in any way interfere with the established churches. This was remarkably modest, for Swedenborg wrote that in a trance "The Lord God, the Creator and Redeemer of the world . . . had chosen me to declare to men the spiritual contents of Scripture; and that He Himself would declare to me what I should write on the subject." Those who believe themselves to be the appointed of God usually try to found their own religion. Swedenborg didn't even encourage others to take up conversations with the spirits. He warned that anybody who tried could easily be deceived by evil spirits. The high moral standards Swedenborg preached were entirely in conformity with the accepted morality of his day.

Swedenborg believed that men could continue to worship in the conventional manner and still accept his visions. A few years after his death, however, some of those who had been impressed by his works established a church based upon his teachings. The first of these churches, called the Church of the New Jerusalem, was founded in England in 1792. A Swedenborg church was organized in America a few years later.

Swedenborgian churches still exist today. Like Swedenborg himself, his followers are not aggressive proselytizers. They have made few attempts to translate the master's difficult and obscure doctrines into an idiom that might be grasped by large numbers of people. However, Swedenborgianism has had an influence far beyond the numbers who have actually belonged to Swedenborgian churches.

Most of the weighty volumes that Swedenborg produced during his "illuminated" years—and he turned out about one a year—are virtually unreadable. The philosopher Immanuel Kant, who was hardly a lively stylist himself, found Swedenborg's books very heavy going, and advised his friends against bothering with them. Kant had a particular interest in Swedenborg, for some of the Swedish seer's theories paralleled his own. This distressed Kant, for he doubted Swedenborg's sanity.

"The system of Swedenborg," wrote Kant, "is unfortunately very similar to my own philosophy. It is not impossible that my rational views may be considered absurd because of that affinity. As to the offensive comparison I declare we must either suppose greater intelligence and truth at the basis of Swedenborg's writings that the first impression excites, or that it is a mere accident when he coincides with my system."

Much of Swedenborg's theological and philosophical system is of no concern to us here. But his belief that there was an invisible world in which the spirits of the dead carried on a rather down-to-earth sort of existence, and that he at least could break through the barrier to that other world, is of great interest. Swedenborg was more influential than any other individual in reactivating the ancient practice of necromancy or conversing with the dead, which formed the basis of modern spiritualism. Swedenborg's example—he was a man who spoke with the dead—counted more than any of his direct teachings.

As already indicated, Swedenborg believed that man lived simultaneously in both an earthly and a spiritual world. After bodily death, the spiritual part of man survived, though spiritual in nature, retained the appearance of the earthly body. Upon death the spirit proceeded to a sort of halfway world between earth and heaven and hell. This halfway world resembled the earthly world, so closely that it took a while for the dead to realize that they really were dead. At this point they met all of their friends and relatives from earth, either dead or alive.

After becoming accustomed to the fact that they are spirits, the newly dead choose either heaven or hell according to their nature. Those who on earth had led conventionally good lives —loved God and their fellow men, helped the weak and so forth—gravitated naturally to heaven. There they lived with their friends, old and new, in communities that in many ways resembled earthly communities, except that they kept getting better and better. Those in heaven, said Swedenborg, "are continually advancing to the springtime of life and the more thousands of years they live, the more delightful and happy the spring to which they attain, and this to eternity with an increase according to the progressions and degrees of their love, charity, and faith . . ." The angels in Swedenborg's heaven were really the spirits of good men long dead.

Hell, like heaven, was a place where spirits went voluntarily. Those who in life had been addicted to various vices were attracted to hell, a place where every sort of activity was allowed. There were only two restrictions: no one could cultivate a worse vice than he had known on earth, and no one could ever get out. The demons that inflicted tortures on the damned had on earth been sadists, who enjoyed that sort of thing. None of the tortures involved physical pain—Swedenborg was a gentle man—rather, they consisted of horrid hallucinations, phobias, and nightmares.

While the residents of heaven became better and more youthful-looking, "to grow old in heaven is to grow young," those in hell came to resemble the image of their own evil, like the picture of Dorian Gray. "The faces of some are black, others fiery-like torches, others disfigured with pimples, warts, and ulcers, some seem to have no face, but in its stead something hairy, and with some only teeth are seen."

In essence the spiritualists of the nineteenth century adopted Swedenborg's view of heaven. Though being even more inclined to gentleness and optimism than the Swedish seer, they modified his picture of hell or eliminated hell entirely.

Swedenborg's descriptions are very concrete and exact. He insisted to the very last moment of his life that what he said about heaven and hell were not speculations, but things that he had actually seen with his own eyes.

While entranced, Swedenborg traveled not only to the land of the spirits, but also to other planets and reported what he saw there. Of the inhabitants of Venus he says: "They are of two kinds; some are gentle and benevolent, others wild, cruel, and of gigantic stature. The latter rob and plunder and live by this means; the former have so great a degree of gentleness and kindness that they are always beloved by the good; thus they often see the Lord appear in their own form on their earth."

Moon men, according to Swedenborg, "are small, like children of six or seven years old; at the same time they have the strength of men like ourselves. Their voice rolls like thunder, and the sound proceeds from the belly, because the moon is in quite a different atmosphere from the other planets."

Thus Swedenborg not only anticipated spiritualism, but also today's flying saucer cults, where "contactees" regularly report on their visits to other planets, and discussions with the SI's (Space Intelligences).

Imagine for a moment trying to argue or even discuss Swedenborg's visions with him. He would doubtless insist, kindly but firmly, that he knew what he knew because he had seen all those things that he had described. He would then go on, with great earnestness, and at great length to amplify his statements. He was a nice man, but impossible to argue with, and it is small wonder that most of the people of the time simply chose not to press him too closely regarding his visits with the spirits.

Swedenborg is not only known as a mystic and visionary, he also was reputed to possess other psychic abilities. Swedenborg attributed all of his psychic abilities to his talks with the spirits or angels, but modern parapsychologists would say he was clairvoyant (that he possessed the ability to see distant events) and that he was precognitive (he was able to see the future).

Certainly the most famous and well-attested example of Swedenborg's clairvoyance, indeed one of the best cases for clairvoyance in all history, took place in September 1759. Immanuel Kant wrote the most complete version of this incident. Swedenborg was staying at the town of Göteborg. It was Saturday evening, and Swedenborg was with a party of about fifteen persons. Kant wrote: "About six o'clock, Swedenborg went out, and returned to the company quite pale and alarmed. He said that a dangerous fire had just broken out in Stockholm at Södermalm [Göteborg is two hundred and forty miles southwest of Stockholm] and that it was spreading very fast. He was restless, and he went out often. He said that the house of one of his friends, whom he named, was already in ashes, and that his own was in danger. At eight o'clock, after he had been out again, he joyfully exclaimed, 'Thank God! the fire is extinguished, the third door from my house.' This news occasioned great commotion throughout the city, but particularly amongst the company in which he was. It was announced to the governor the same evening. On Sunday morning Swedenborg was summoned to the governor, who questioned him concerning the disaster."

The account continues that it was not until Monday evening, two days after the fire had taken place and had been described by Swedenborg that the people of Göteborg got definite news of the disaster from a messenger bringing letters sent by the Stockholm Board of Trade. The reports were supposed to confirm the details of the fire as they had been reported by Swedenborg.

This incident has been cited over and over again, not only by Swedenborgians, but by all believers in psychic phenomena. It is considered a classic case of clairvoyance, and anyone reading the literature on psychic phenomena is bound to run across the story of Swedenborg and the Stockholm fire sooner or later—usually sooner. The case seems to be incontrovertible evidence of clairvoyance. There were many witnesses who had heard Swedenborg describe the fire; he could not possibly have known about it; his report was detailed enough so that mere chance could not possibly have accounted for it; there was no chance that he could have known about the fire through normal means since Göteborg is more than two hundred miles from Stockholm. But the case also presents some problems which are common to many other cases of alleged psychic phenomena.

How do we know what Swedenborg said about the fire and when? The report on the event was written by Kant, a man noted for his precision. In addition Kant did not like Swedenborg, and would not have been likely to exaggerate his powers as a seer. But Kant himself did not hear Swedenborg's prediction. In fact, he never met Swedenborg. Kant heard the story and wanted to know more about it. A friend of his, an Englishman named Green, was going to Stockholm in 1767, and Kant asked him "to make particular inquiries respecting the miraculous gift which Swedenborg possesses." According to Kant, Green "examined all, not only in Stockholm, but also in Göteborg, where he was well acquainted with the most respectable houses, and where he could obtain the most authentic and complete information."

But Green was still interviewing witnesses ten years after the event. We have no idea who Green interviewed. Were they part of that original party of fifteen who overheard Swedenborg describe the fire, or did they only know of it from hearsay? The only witness whom we know for sure that Green interviewed was Swedenborg himself. Naturally the mystic confirmed all the details of his vision.

Are there any other recorded versions of this incident? Yes, there are two of them, but both are written by Englishmen who based their accounts on what Swedenborg told them. There is therefore not a single firsthand written account by any of those who were supposed to have heard Swedenborg's remarkable visionary statements about a fire so many miles away.

Thus, what looks at first glance to be an air-tight case of Swedenborg's psychic abilities turns out to be nothing of the sort. We do not really know what happened at Göteborg on that Saturday evening in 1759. There is no evidence that the incident was in any way distorted or faked by Swedenborg, or indeed that it did not happen exactly the way he said it did. The verdict in this case, as in so many others in this area, must simply be "unproved" and since more than two hundred years have passed since the events described, we must also conclude that it is unprovable.

A second striking incident involving Swedenborg's alleged psychic powers took place toward the end of 1761. Swedenborg had been summoned to the court by Queen Louisa Ulrica. Naturally, she had heard of his powers, and asked him if he could get a message from her brother, who had died just that year. Swedenborg said that he could. But the next time he appeared at court the Queen seemed to have forgotten the commission she had given him. She was playing cards with some of the ladies of the court when Swedenborg approached and said that he had a message for her. The Queen asked him to repeat it, but he said that it was much too private. The two went off together, and when the Queen returned she looked very pale and shaken. She said, "This no mortal could have told me!"

There are several versions of this incident, and they differ in small details. In one Swedenborg delivered the message immediately after having been asked, without the delay of a week. The words the Queen is said to have uttered after hearing Swedenborg also differ. All the accounts, however, seem to be traceable either to the Queen or to Swedenborg himself.

What message Swedenborg delivered to the Queen is unknown. The Queen was a Prussian by birth and Sweden and Prussia had recently been at war. Many suspected that the message had to do with the Queen's relationship to Prussia during the war. But neither Swedenborg nor the Queen would say what had passed between them, and they are the only possible judges as to how extraordinary Swedenborg's information was.

The incident is striking and dramatic—a secret message to a queen is the stuff of historical novels—but it does not make very good evidence for communication with the dead. Clearly the Queen thought she had received a message from her dead brother, but there are too many cases of similar "messages" turning out to be purely the product of wishful thinking on the part of the receiver. Without knowing the exact contents of this message from the dead, we can hardly make a judgment on it.

Assume for a moment that Swedenborg did deliver some sort of extraordinary message. How could it be accounted for? Swedenborg said he obtained it by talking directly with the spirit of the dead man, and most spiritualists would agree with that explanation. Those who are interested in psychic phenomena, but shy away from strictly spiritualist explanations, might say that Swedenborg picked up the message from the mind of the Queen herself by telepathy.

Still a third celebrated story of Swedenborg's psychic abilities concerns his location of a lost receipt. According to Kant's account, the widow of the Dutch ambassador was being sued for payment of a bill for some expensive silverware. She was sure that her husband had already paid the bill before his death, but she was unable to locate the receipt. She asked Swedenborg to talk directly to her husband's spirit and find out where he had put it. Swedenborg did so, and was told that the missing receipt was in a secret drawer in his desk, where it was located after a brief search.

Kant's version of the incident was again supplied by his informant Green. But there are other versions of this case—at least eleven other versions. There are so many contradictions between them that one must view this entire story with suspicion.

One final story concerns Swedenborg's prediction of the day of his own death. Early in 1772 the great theologian John Wesley received a letter from Swedenborg. The seer said that he knew Wesley was most anxious to see him, and that he would be happy to comply with this wish at any time. One of those who was with Wesley, the Reverend Samuel Smith, tells the story:

"Mr. Wesley frankly acknowledged to the company that he had been very strongly impressed with the desire to see and converse with Swedenborg, and that he had never mentioned that desire to anyone.

"Mr. Wesley wrote for answer, that he was closely occupied in preparing for a six months' journey, but would do himself the pleasure of waiting upon Mr. Swedenborg soon after his return to London.

"Swedenborg wrote in reply, that the visit proposed by Mr. Wesley would be too late, as he, Swedenborg, should go into the world of spirits on the 29th day of the next month [March] never more to return."

Swedenborg died March 29, 1772, one month after he wrote to Wesley.

The story is, however, more dramatically than scientifically satisfying. The original correspondence between Swedenborg and Wesley, if any, has been lost, and there is simply no other confirming evidence as to whether this incident really took place.

For all Swedenborg's insistence on the concreteness and exactness of his statements, they turn out to be as ephemeral as those of other mystics.

CHAPTER VI

Mesmer and the Magnetizers

YOU MIGHT BE A BIT SURPRISED to find Friedrich (more commonly Franz) Anton Mesmer, the black sheep "father of hypnotism," listed among the "Masters of the Occult." During the last century or so Mesmer has been more or less rehabilitated. And, mesmerism or animal magnetism, now renamed hypnotism, has become a subject for respectable scientific research and discussion.

As often happens when the mystery is removed from a subject, hypnotism has been steadily melting away under the cold glare of scientific investigation, and today there are many scientists and physicians who doubt there is really such a thing as a "hypnotic state." Surely the image of the Svengali type of hypnotist with the glowing eyes, who can control his victim's every move, has been shattered beyond repair.

Perhaps because hypnotism has become so stuffy and respectable, it isn't well remembered today how much of spiritualism, and the modern belief in psychic phenomena, indeed most of modern occultism, has been filtered through the work of Mesmer and his followers. The beliefs themselves have been around in one form or another through all of human history. The needs and desires that created them are an eternal part of the human condition. Each age simply shapes these beliefs into a form acceptable to the time, and explains them in contemporary language. So it was Mesmer who gave his age an acceptable framework for the belief that the universe was permeated with an invisible power which could be manipulated by certain techniques, and by certain individuals to control human activity, particularly health and illness. Religious mystics attributed this mysterious power to God. Rationalist mystics (the terms are not necessarily contradictory) of the seventeenth and eighteenth centuries looked for subtile fluids, forces, and essences. The very same beliefs flourish today among the followers of Edgar Cayce, Oral Roberts, and multitude of tent-show faith healers.

Mesmer's disciples picked up another thread of occultism—the belief that a trance state (a state of altered consciousness we might call it today) can put one in touch with some other and presumably better world. The entranced person is believed to have a clearer vision of the universe, and of universes which are invisible to a person through normal sensory channels. The extraordinary publicity given to a seance in which the late Bishop James A. Pike was supposed to have been put in contact with his dead son through the agency of the medium Arthur Ford, and at least part of the current fascination with L.S.D. and other hallucinogenic drugs, are indications of our continuing interest in trances.

Mesmer was born in Iznang, Austria, on May 23, 1734. He was a leisurely student. First he took a degree in philosophy, then studied law, and finally graduated from the medical school of the University of Vienna. His thesis was written on the subject of "The Influence of the Planets on the Human Body." It was sort of a combination of medicine and astrology. Underlying the thesis was the concept that the universe, everything from stars to the human body, radiated or somehow gave off a powerful force or fluid that affected every other object in the universe. The nature of this force or fluid and the methods by which it could be controlled were only vaguely described. Later, when he became world-famous, Mesmer was to date his whole theory of animal magnetism back to this school thesis. However, there was virtually nothing original in Mesmer's thesis. It was borrowed wholesale from mystical and medical speculation of earlier times, particularly from the writings of that oddball genius Paracelsus.

Mesmer's ideas sound strange and quackish to us today. They certainly were not part of the mainstream of theory and research that led to modern medical practice. But in the eighteenth century, theories which linked astrology with medicine were still reasonably respectable, and Mesmer began a regular medical practice in Vienna.

It is hard to escape the conclusion, however, that Mesmer was a man with his eye always on the main chance. He enjoyed the good life and did not care to overwork himself. After practicing medicine for a few years Mesmer married a rich widow ten years his senior. Though he later claimed that he had spent this period testing his magnetic theories, it seems that he spent the bulk of his time in pursuit of fashion and the arts. From all accounts he appears to have been a charming and cultured man, though inclined to irascibility. Portraits show him to have been good-looking, in the fleshy sort of way popular during that era. He looks rather like his contemporary Casanova. Perhaps the words "magnetic personality" have never been more appropriately applied than to Mesmer. He was socially successful and numbered among his friends such celebrities of the music world as Mozart, Gluck, and Haydn.

But Mesmer had not abandoned either his medical practice or the old Paracelsian idea of universal forces or fluids, and their effects upon the human body. At about this time the Englishman John Canton discovered how to make artificial magnets. The physical sciences, physics, and chemistry had made enormous strides during the seventeenth and eighteenth centuries. Impressed by the discoveries in the physical sciences, many physicians began to apply them to medicine, in a rather heavy-handed way. All manner of electrical cures became popular. Magnetism seemed even more promising than electricity, for Paracelsus had often written of "magnetism," though he probably used the word metaphorically.

Father Maximilian Hell, one of the Empress Maria Theresa of Austria's court astrologers, was most interested in magnets. He lent some magnetic plates to his friend Dr. Mesmer to try on a patient.

Despite Mesmer's claims that he had been working on animal magnetism for years, the first record of a case in which he applied the magnetic cure was for July 28, 1774. The patient was a Fraulein Franzel Oesterline, who suffered from recurring attacks of convulsions, headaches, delirium, vomiting, and partial paralysis. None of the conventional treatments of the day seemed to help at all.

Coming to Fraulein Oesterline while she was in the first stages of an attack, Mesmer laid the magnetic plates on her body. She immediately went into furious convulsions, but these lasted only a few moments. Then the attack subsided, although under ordinary circumstances such attacks lasted for hours.

On the following day, at the onset of another attack Mesmer again successfully applied the magnets. After a few more treatments the attacks came to an end, at least temporarily.

Then Mesmer began what was to prove to be a long and fruitless search for recognition of his treatment by the medical establishment. Several months later Fraulein Oesterline suffered a relapse. Mesmer invited the scientist Jan Ingenhousz, a member of the Royal Academy of London, to observe the magnetic cure. When Ingenhousz left, Mesmer thought he was satisfied with what he had seen, but two days later the scientist denounced the magnetic cure as a "ridiculous, prearranged fraud."

Mesmer became embroiled in a controversy of another sort. Father Hell, who had lent Mesmer the magnets, now claimed that the magnetic cure was his invention and a bitter controversy broke out between the two. Throughout his career Mesmer showed a genius for getting involved in bitter public controversies. The argument with Father Hell doubtless accounts for Mesmer's strenuous efforts to prove a prior claim to the theory of animal magnetism.

Though Mesmer was a controversial figure, the fame of his "cures" spread, and the patients flocked to him. Ultimately Mesmer got into real trouble over the case of Maria Theresa Paradis, an eighteen-year-old pianist who had been blind from the age of four.

The girl, a favorite of the Empress Maria Theresa (after whom she had been named), had been treated by many famous physicians, including the Empress' own personal doctor. These treatments had been extensive, often very painful, and worthless. Mesmer declared that the girl's loss of eyesight was due to hysteria, and said that he could cure her.

Today hysteria is used as a general term to describe an extreme degree of psychological agitation, which under some conditions might result in hysterical blindness, paralysis, or other physical symptoms. But in Mesmer's day hysteria was thought to be entirely physical in origin. It was considered strictly a woman's disease which resulted from an affliction of the womb. The word hysteria itself comes from *hysteron,* the Greek word for uterus.

Mesmer took the young pianist into his home, a tactical error as it turned out, for it gave his opponents a fertile field in which to spread rumors of immorality. When Mesmer reported that the girl had regained her eyesight the members of the Faculty of Medicine in Vienna rushed to examine her. The medical establishment was thoroughly hostile to Mesmer, and the doctors doubtless delighted to discover that, despite Mesmer's claim, the girl was still blind. The physicians reported that the girl only "imagined" that she could see. They also threatened to recommend that the Empress discontinue the girl's pension unless she departed from Mesmer's house at once. After the Faculty of Medicine's report Mesmer sadly announced that the girl had "relapsed" into her former state of blindness. (In fairness to Mesmer it must be said that while his treatments often didn't work, orthodox eighteenth-century medicine wasn't very good either. At least Mesmer did no harm while other physicians regularly bled or purged their patients to death.)

Vienna was no longer a comfortable place for Mesmer. His license to practice medicine was revoked and he may actually have been ordered out of the country. When Mesmer left Vienna he left his wife behind. He spent a year or so traveling about Europe and finally in 1778 he came to Paris to start a practice based on "magnetic cures." He set up his *clinique* in an elegant mansion on the Place Vendôme, and in the frantic and decadent atmosphere of prerevolutionary France, Mesmer flourished. The patients and the money poured in.

Mesmer was genuinely interested in getting scientific investigation and recognition of his work. But he had as little success with the Faculty of Medicine in Paris as he had in Vienna. However, Mesmer made one convert on the Faculty, Maurice D'Eslon. In September 1780, D'Eslon called a meeting of his colleagues in order to have the learned men listen to an explanation of Mesmer's ideas. Mesmer had written out a list of twenty-seven vaguely worded "propositions concerning animal magnetism" which D'Eslon read to the hostile group. On Mesmer's behalf D'Eslon proposed that a test be made of the magnetic treatment. Twenty-four patients would be chosen, half would be treated by orthodox methods, the other half by Mesmer's methods, to see which group would recover first. There are grave shortcomings to such a test, but still it seems like an honest attempt to cooperate with a scientific investigation. The Faculty of Medicine was in no mood for such a test and brushed aside the proposal. Moreover, they warned D'Eslon that if he did not stop fooling around with those strange "cures" his name would be stricken from the rolls. D'Eslon persisted, and was expelled, becoming, in the eyes of his supporters, a martyr for mesmerism.

Despite continued rejection by the professionals, Mesmer and his "cures" had become all the rage, if not among the common people, then at least among those wealthy enough to pay his fees. Mesmer created so much excitement in the fashionable world that on behalf of the King he was offered a pension of 20,000 livres, and a further sum of 10,000 livres annually to provide him with a suitable house. The condition was that Mesmer would establish a school in which he was to teach the "secrets" of his treatment. The offer was a generous one, but Mesmer rejected it for he said to be party to such a bargain would be beneath the dignity of the great truth he proclaimed. It is fair to guess that the offer was simply not large enough to satisfy his greed. He was already collecting enormous fees from his patients and the royal pension might actually result in a loss of income.

Two years after the royal offer was rejected Mesmer delivered a series of lectures on his system. The wealthy students who attended his lectures paid considerably more than the King had offered. Mesmer encouraged his students to go out into the provinces and establish magnetic treatment centers of their own. However, there were two conditions that had to be agreed to before attending the master's course. First, all students had to swear that they would never, under any circumstances, reveal the secrets of mesmerism. They also had to agree to turn over to Mesmer half of all fees they received. Since most of Mesmer's pupils were already men of great wealth the money meant little to them. These pupils formed a Society of Harmony, which despite its name was immediately engulfed in fierce squabbles. Shortly this group of unruly disciples broke with Mesmer, and with one another.

By the time Mesmer came to Paris his treatment had changed considerably from the days when he first borrowed Father Hell's magnets. Mesmer had abandoned the magnets entirely after meeting Dr. Johann Joseph Gassner, a celebrated healer who was accomplishing cures merely by making mysterious motions with his hands and staring into the patient's eyes. Though Mesmer coined the term animal magnetism to describe the healing force or fluid supposedly controlled by his treatment, it had little to do with magnetism as we know it; in fact, it had little to do with animals. Animal magnetism might be translated as vital force or fluid. Mesmer's animal magnetism was simply another manifestation of the ancient mystical belief in a universal force or fluid that permeated the universe and controlled everything from stars to the lowliest living creature. By watching Gassner, Mesmer concluded that the magnets themselves were not necessary, but that the necessary element was the magnetizer himself, who controlled the fluid by his techniques. Mesmer may have believed, though he never explicitly said so, that the will of the magnetizer was an active agency in directing the flow of animal magnetism. The will of the magnetizer may actually have been "the secret" of animal magnetism that Mesmer guarded so jealously.

Mesmer had become heir to a great and still very active healing tradition, the laying on of hands. Practically every society has believed that there are certain individuals who have the power to cure disease by a touch of the hand. In the West such beliefs go back at least to Biblical times, and probably well before that. Usually the healer was a priest or a member of royalty. In England the idea that the King's touch could heal certain diseases began with Edward the Confessor in the eleventh century. But it hung on well into a period in which any belief in the King as an object of divine power should have disappeared. Charles II, who reigned in the seventeenth century, vigorously revived the custom and performed some hundred thousand "treatments" during his reign.

The thoroughly cynical Charles certainly had no belief in his own powers as a healer but merely used the ceremony as a political ploy to impress the masses. With the words, "I touch you. God heals you," the afflicted man was given a silver coin called a "touchpiece" and presumed cured. Those who had the temerity to remain ill were told that they did not have enough faith. The King, you see, was always right.

William III hated the custom, which he considered a vile superstition. Yet he was unable to eliminate the ceremony entirely. To the sick he would growl, "May God give you better health and more sense."

About a century before Mesmer began his cures there was a celebrated healer named Valentine Greatrakes operating in England. By merely stroking the afflicted part of the body with his hand, Greatrakes had great, though far from universal success in alleviating pain and curing many different diseases. He was a sincere and religious man who never accepted a fee for his cures, and indeed invested an enormous amount of his own time and energy into performing them.

Greatrakes himself thought that his healing power was "an extraordinary gift of God." He believed disease to be the result of possession by demons who were driven out by his hands. Scientists, including the hardheaded Robert Boyle, were impressed by the healer's success, though they sought other explanations for it. They postulated some sort of "effulgent aura" that had curative powers.

Mesmer combined ancient traditions with up-to-date jargon about "magnetic fluids." It was all very effective. Mesmer was a showman as well as a healer and did not content himself with a simple "laying on of hands." In Mesmer's *clinique* the doctor employed all the regalia and ritual of a sorcerer.

In the center of the room stood Mesmer's celebrated *baquet,* a large wooden tub, filled with bottles of "magnetic water." From the tub radiated iron rods that were supposed to direct the "magnetic rays." Patients were able to touch the afflicted parts of their bodies to the rods.

The patients themselves stood around the *baquet* in a circle. They would either touch hands to form a "magnetic ring" or actually be tied lightly together with a cord. Lights would be dimmed and soft music played. Slowly the mood began to take hold of the patients. Some began to laugh uncontrollably while others broke into tears. They trembled and sweated profusely. Mesmer's assistants would pass among them touching those who still held their emotions in check with "magnetic rods."

Into the midst of this increasingly frenzied scene would step Mesmer himself, wearing a lavender robe embroidered with golden flowers, and carrying a wand. As he walked from patient to patient, Mesmer would sometimes touch one on the head with his wand and sometimes gaze deeply into the eyes of another. The actions of the patients became more violent. They screamed, vomited, began spitting blood, and went into furious convulsions. This was "the magnetic crisis," the moment of treatment Mesmer considered absolutely essential to cure. Afterwards the patients usually collapsed from sheer exhaustion. When he had recovered, a patient was likely to say that he felt much better.

The frenzies that Mesmer's magnetic treatment produced are not unusual. They can be seen at revival meetings throughout the country today, and should not have been unfamiliar to eighteenth-century Paris. Yet Mesmer's fame gripped the city almost like a mania. His clients and admirers included such astute men as Lafayette and many of the most eminent literary figures, politicians, and aristocrats of the day. Mesmer was known as "the great enchanter" and the gold poured into his coffers in a steady stream. In a single year Mesmer collected over 400,000 francs in fees.

The King, who had first wished to sponsor the Viennese healer, was now becoming a bit alarmed about him. Mesmer's increasing wealth, his arrogance, and the spectacle of some of the most important men in France screaming and twitching around Mesmer's *baquet* must have been disturbing. Finally, with royal encouragement, two different commissions were set up to study Mesmer and his method. The commission appointed by the Faculty of Medicine included several leading figures from different sciences. One was Benjamin Franklin, then seventy-eight years old and serving as the American ambassador to France. Franklin was universally respected for his scientific acumen. Other members of the commission were Antoine Lavoisier, the discoverer of oxygen, Jean Sylvain Bailly, the astronomer, and a certain Dr. Joseph Guillotin, who gave his name to a particular labor-saving device that was shortly to become very popular in France. Ironically, both Lavoisier and Bailly were destined to die on the instrument named after the ingenious Dr. Guillotin.

Mesmer was finally about to get the scientific investigation he had longed for, but he had apparently given up all hope of scientific recognition. Whereas on previous occasions he had cooperated fully with investigators, this time he would not cooperate at all. Mesmer may well have doubted that he could get a fair hearing before either commission. His previous experience with scientific commissions had not been happy. He may also have feared that an investigation would harm his lucrative practice. Without Mesmer to study, the commissioners had to find a substitute, and they turned to his old supporter D'Eslon. D'Eslon and Mesmer had quarreled, but D'Eslon still clung fiercely to Mesmer's theories, and had a thriving magnetic *clinique* of his own in Paris. D'Eslon, a true believer in animal magnetism, welcomed the investigators, convinced that they would confirm the value of the magnetic treatments. Ironically, D'Eslon died while being mesmerized in August 1786.

The nature of the commission's inquiry has often been misunderstood, and its findings unfairly criticized. The inquiry was very limited in nature. The investigators were looking solely for evidence of the magnetic fluid. The investigators were wise enough to know that they could not accurately judge the effectiveness of the cure. Even today, with much greater medical knowledge and sophisticated testing techniques, it remains extremely difficult to discover whether this or that course of treatment is successful. Part of the difficulty is that the physical effects of a treatment must be separated from the purely psychological effects. Besides, pressing this inquiry too closely might have meant annoying some of D'Eslon's wealthy and powerful patients.

The commission was ingenious in its attempts to find the magnetic fluid. In one of the tests D'Eslon came to Franklin's house and "magnetized" a tree in his yard. The subject—a twelve-year-old boy—was brought into the garden blindfolded and led from tree to tree. In front of one of the trees he developed convulsions and collapsed. Unfortunately, it was not the magnetized tree—he had never gotten within twenty-five feet of that.

The inquiry was a frustrating one and in the end the commissioners concluded that they could perceive no evidence of the hypothetical magnetic fluid. They were also rather upset by the violent antics of the patients undergoing the magnetic crisis, and said that in such a state a patient might cause serious harm to himself or others. Confidentially the commissioners emphasized the dangers of the magnetic treatment and recommended its legal suppression.

However, the commissioners were not entirely blind to the fact that something, though they were not quite sure what, was happening as a result of Mesmer's magnetic treatment.

"All [the patients] are subject to the person who magnetized them. If to every appearance they lie completely exhausted, the eye or the voice of the magnetizer soon brings them out of their swoon. There is undoubtedly some power at work, a power that influences men's actions and dominates them. This is the power of the magnetizer himself."

The report continued: "That which has been proved throughout our examination of magnetism is that it can affect man . . . almost at will by stimulating the imagination."

A second report on Mesmerism by the Royal Society of Medicine was made public a few days later. This report arrived at essentially the same conclusions as had the report of the Faculty of Medicine. However, one of the members of the Royal Society's commission, a Monsieur de Jussieu, was mightily impressed by what he had seen. According to M. de Jussieu there was indeed a magnetic fluid that he called "animal heat." It was in his view a very special sort of fluid and therefore could not be detected by the instruments of science.

In fact, M. de Jussieu accepted almost the entire Mesmer doctrine of animal magnetism, with one important exception. The exception concerned the power of the magnetizer. In Mesmer's own writings the magnetizer appears merely as a transmitter of the magnetic fluid—he seems almost incidental to the process. But de Jussieu held that the real power of the magnetic treatment was the will of the magnetizer which controlled and directed the magnetic fluid. Most magnetizers quickly adopted this theory. It became so popular that some of Mesmer's own disciples claimed that the master himself had believed in the supreme importance of the will and that this was the secret which he revealed only to the trusted few. It may have been.

From this sort of theorizing came the popular vision of the Svengali-like wizard who could control his subjects by the operation of his will alone. A physical or electrical force seemed to emanate from the fingertips or eyes of the fictional magnetizer. Some of the early subjects of animal magnetism actually reported seeing and feeling this radiant force. Even today the idea persists that only a person with a "strong will" can be a hypnotist, and that a hypnotized person somehow has a "weaker" will than the hypnotist.

Condemnation by two powerful scientific committees was more than Mesmer could take. He angrily left Paris and returned to his birthplace at Iznang. His many friends and admirers in France tried to lure him back, but without success. Mesmer's pride had been badly hurt, and he seemed to lack the energy or desire to carry on a protracted battle with the scientific establishment. Perhaps at some point Mesmer might have returned to Paris to pick up his career, but the French Revolution began, and people had little time for the study of his esoteric science.

Mesmer himself continued to live on quietly, first at Iznang and then in Vienna. During the French Revolution Mesmer made a casual remark that the revolutionaries were perhaps not as bad as the Austrians thought. Austria was at that time gripped by an antirevolutionary hysteria, and when the remark was repeated to the police by someone who overheard it, Mesmer was branded a subversive and ordered out of the country.

Mesmer moved on to Switzerland, the traditional homeland of European exiles. There he stayed for almost twenty years, mostly in the town of Fraunfeld near Zürich. First he supported himself as a country doctor. After the Revolution the French government reimbursed Mesmer for some of the property he had lost during the upheavals by granting him a pension. Mesmer was able to retire from active practice and devote himself to his favorite hobby of music.

Despite repeated scientific denunciations mesmerism itself was flourishing throughout Europe. Had Mesmer desired it he might again have become a prominent and controversial figure, but he seemed to prefer the obscurity of a little Swiss village. During the first decade of the nineteenth century most of those who practiced mesmerism and praised its namesake were quite unaware that Mesmer himself was still alive. "The Great Enchanter" died in Meersburg on March 5, 1815, at the age of eighty-one.

Long before Mesmer died the leadership of the movement which was identified with his name had passed from his hands. Even while he was in Paris, Mesmer had broken with most of his disciples, who had gone on to set up rival centers for the study and practice of mesmerism. When the practice of mesmerism was picked up again after the Revolution, it was under a new set of leaders, who often held very different theories and aims than Mesmer himself.

Stefan Zweig, the German novelist and one of Mesmer's biographers, wrote of him: "It is always an intellectual tragedy, when a discovery is more brilliant than its discoverer . . . That is what happened in Mesmer's case. He was the first to meet one of the most important problems of modern times, and he had advanced it a considerable way."

The next important figure in the growth of mesmerism, magnetism, or hypnotism was the Marquis de Puységur, a wealthy nobleman who in 1784 had paid Mesmer a large sum of money to learn the secrets of animal magnetism. Puységur then retired to his estates near Soissons in order to practice his new techniques on the local peasants.

On the evening of May 4, 1784, Puységur was magnetizing a young peasant named Victor, whom he hoped to cure of a mild case of pleurisy. The event turned out to be as important as Mesmer's magnetic treatment of Fraulein Oesterline. Puységur's technique was to touch the afflicted area with his hand and then wave his hand in front of the subject's face while staring intently into his eyes. After a few moments of this treatment, Victor fell soundly asleep. But it was no ordinary sleep, for Victor could hear the Puységur's voice and responded quickly and rather eerily to his suggestions. When Victor began talking in his sleep about something that worried him, Puységur suggested that he concentrate on something more pleasant. This the young peasant did, and he began going through the motions of taking part in a shooting match. When Victor awoke he said he felt better but could remember nothing of what had happened while he was asleep.

Today the popular conception of the hypnotized or mesmerized subject is that of the somnambulist, the person who in a sleep-like trance responds to the commands of the hypnotist. However, Mesmer's subjects went into twitching, screaming convulsions. Though Mesmer seemed to have some ability to direct the course of these convulsions he was not otherwise able to order his subjects around. Mesmer believed that this violent crisis was absolutely necessary for the healing of a patient through the operation of animal magnetism. The commissioners who investigated the treatments found the violent crisis distasteful, and quite possibly dangerous. Puységur himself disliked the convulsions and was delighted to be able to carry out further experiments with animal magnetism without inducing the crisis in his patients. It was Puységur who coined the term somnambulist, or artificial sleepwalker.

Victor, the first somnambulist, was an excellent subject,

and Puységur put him into a magnetic sleep repeatedly. The Marquis noted that when Victor was awake, he was the most stupid of men, but when in a magnetic sleep his intelligence seemed to change entirely. "I have met no one more profound, wiser, or more clear-sighted than he." Moreover, Victor seemed to respond not only to Puységur's spoken commands, but to unspoken ones as well—the magnetizer seemed to be able to communicate with his subject telepathically.

"I have no need of speaking to him. When I think in his presence he seems to hear me and replies. When someone comes into the room Victor sees him only if I will him to, when Victor converses with him he says only what I will him to say, not exactly what I silently dictate but what the meaning requires. When he starts to say more than I consider prudent for others to hear, then I can cut short his very sentences in the middle of a word and can change his thoughts altogether."

Even more spectacular effects were noticed in other magnetized subjects. Some of the somnambulists seemed able to diagnose their own ailments and prescribe for them. They also claimed the power to see inside of others and thus diagnose and prescribe for them with what many believed to be uncanny accuracy. A few somnambulists revealed the ability to diagnose patients who were not present merely by holding a lock of their hair, a paper with their handwriting, or some object which the patient had handled recently. The cures prescribed by the somnambulists were usually simple herbal remedies, and usually harmless, though one of these magnetized healers once prescribed a dose of sleeping powder for herself that was strong enough, according to a doctor, "to put four strong men asleep forever."

The cult of the sleeping healer was nothing new in history.

As far back as Pharaohnic Egypt there had been temples dedicated to the gods of medicine. The sick would often sleep in these temples, and in their dreams the god was supposed to prescribe the proper cure for their ailment. The ancient belief continues to this day. Witness the fantastic popularity of Edgar Cayce. Though Cayce is today known mostly for his prophetic and other occult utterances, while alive he was famous primarily for being a healer. He would apparently go to sleep and while in this state describe in homey and vague terms the progress of a person's illness and prescribe a cure. The cures were also simple, homey, and generally harmless. They were probably also useless, but belief in Cayce or any other healer will in itself be a powerful curative element. Cayce would have in no way seemed unfamiliar to Puységur and other magnetists of his day.

Various sorts of "eyeless vision"—that is, seeing with parts of the body other than the eyes—were demonstrated by somnambulists. For example, magnetized subjects seemed able to identify objects placed on their stomachs. Traveling clairvoyance, the reputed ability to see distant objects and events, was also repeatedly encountered, and entranced subjects described what was supposed to be happening miles away.

All of these apparently remarkable occurrences were later lumped together as "the higher phenomena," those events for which no physical explanation could readily be found. But the early magnetists, particularly the French like Puységur, resolutely denied that there was anything nonmaterial about any of these effects, no matter how strange they appeared to be. All, they said, could be explained by the properties of the theoretical magnetic fluid. The magnetists were forced to stretch their magnetic fluid pretty far to have it cover all the phenomena observed. The theory of animal magnetism was continually being revised and reworked and renamed to cover "the higher phenomena," but in the end it just wouldn't fit anymore.

Animal magnetism, mesmerism, or whatever was distinctly under a scientific cloud for most of the nineteenth century. Even the name was a source of endless controversy. Every practitioner had his own theory about how the process worked, and most had their own pet names for it. Aside from the familiar animal magnetism and mesmerism there were such names as electrobiology, electropsychology, etherology, mental alchemy, and pathetism. Finally in 1840 the Scottish physician Dr. James Braid, one of the few men in England to take the subject seriously, proposed the name "neurypnosis" meaning "sleep of the nervous system." This was later shortened to hypnosis and that name stuck.

Mesmer and his immediate followers like Puységur and D'Eslon were probably about one half scientist and one half mystic, not an unusual combination for the eighteenth century, and not an unknown combination even today. They had hit upon something that they did not understand. These men of the eighteenth century lacked the patience and the intelligence to proceed by the slow and often frustrating method of scientific test and investigation. They sought a short cut to the cure of disease. They were overimpressed by the apparent powers of hypnotism, and this tendency to attribute too much to hypnosis continues to this day. As a matter of fact, the subject of hypnotism has proved to be an extraordinarily difficult one to investigate scientifically.

In Germany and the northern countries and in Russia, scientists regarded animal magnetism as a real and important phenomena, and experimented with it openly, though they did little to advance scientific knowledge in the field. In

France, where mesmerism had first flourished, the scientific community was much more cautious. By 1831 another commission was appointed by the Royal Academy of Medicine to investigate animal magnetism. This commission decided that there really was something to the subject, but they could not say what that something was. English scientists remained openly hostile until a fairly late date, and magnetism did not begin to catch on in the United States until the middle of the nineteenth century.

Ironically it was the Scotsman James Braid, who practiced in England where the subject was held in such low esteem, who made the greatest single contribution toward understanding the subject. Braid proposed not only a new name for the phenomena, but an explanation for it that is still generally accepted today. Braid discounted magnetic fluids and vital forces. He even did away with the will of the magnetizer. According to Braid, the key to hypnosis lies in the mental state of the subject, not in any power that radiates from the hypnotist. People in a hypnotic state are abnormally suggestible and thus can be cured of certain nervous diseases by suggestion. Braid's colleagues did not immediately acclaim his theories, partly because the whole subject of hypnotism was distasteful to them and partly because Braid himself relied heavily on the pseudo science of phrenology (study of bumps on the head) to explain some of the effects of hypnotism. Braid's recognition had to wait half a century until other researchers confirmed many of his theories.

No theory of suggestion, however, could explain "the higher phenomena" like clairvoyance. Braid was a broad-minded man who did not reject them out of hand. He simply had never been able to produce any of them himself during his painstakingly careful experiments, "although I have tried to do so." Still he did not "consider it fair or proper to impugn the statements of others in this matter, who are known to be men of talent and observation."

Since those who followed Braid in the scientific investigation of hypnotism were equally unable to produce "the higher phenomena," "the higher phenomena" were gradually forgotten by scientists. But this does not mean that they disappeared, no indeed. They continued to be produced in ever more exotic forms by the large mystical branch of the magnetist movement.

The interpretation that this branch of the movement placed upon "the higher phenomena" was that they offered convincing proof of the truth of some basic religious ideas, particularly of the nonmaterial nature of part of man and of the immortality of the soul. Wrote Tarday de Montravel in 1785: "If the spirituality of the soul needs a fresh proof, magnetic somnambulism furnishes one such as even the most obstinate materialist can scarcely refuse to recognize."

J. P. F. Deleuze was a French biologist and one of the most important figures in the early history of animal magnetism. He first became interested in the subject in 1785 and his interest continued undiminished until his death at the age of eighty-two in 1833. For years Deleuze was the leading expert on the subject and he valiantly sought to counter the grandiose claims advanced by the mystic magnetists. Still he could not shake off these claims entirely, and he did find some of their evidence impressive. Deleuze concluded that if a person in a hypnotic trance could receive impressions apart from the normal organs of sense and thought, through what we would today call extrasensory perception, then a great truth would be established.

"Once this principle is recognized, the only argument

against the immortality of the soul is discounted. I do not assert that this alone is sufficient to demonstrate the immortality of the soul, but it materially strengthens other proofs by removing all the difficulties. In short, it is much to have incontrovertibly established that the soul can feel, think, know, and reason without the aid of the bodily organs; and that those organs, which in its ordinary state it uses as its instruments, often prove obstacles to the knowledge which it can acquire by immediate perception untainted by transmission through the organs of sense."

Between the years 1829 and 1833, when he died, Deleuze conducted a lengthy correspondence with Dr. G. P. Billot, who had become the leading exponent of a nonmaterialist, religious interpretation of "the higher phenomena" of magnetism. Gradually, over the years, Deleuze inched closer and closer to Billot's position. Finally in one of the last letters the octogenarian Deleuze wrote he proclaimed triumphantly: "I have unlimited confidence in you [Billot], and cannot doubt the truth of your observations. You seem to me destined to effect a change in the ideas generally held on animal magnetism. I should like to live long enough to see the happy revolution, and to thank Heaven for having been introduced into the world of angels."

How very familiar it all sounds. Practically the very same words were spoken by the early scientific adherents of spiritualism, who were convinced that the phenomena produced in the dark seance rooms were absolute proof of the nonmaterial nature of the soul of man, thus of the immortality of the soul. The early founders of psychical research expressed much the same hopes and confidences. Today, nearly a century and a half after the exchange between Deleuze and Billot, the situation regarding "the higher phenomena" has changed hardly at all. Allen Spraggett, one of the leading spokesmen of the current revival of interest in the psychic, has written:

"Now, if man's mind—the source of his psychic powers—is nonmaterial this fact has implications. It prompts the question: why should this nonmaterial element of man die? . . . If the nonmaterial part of man can, because of its nature, theoretically survive death, this gives empirical evidence for communication by the dead a new significance."

The search for some sort of ironclad proof that man somehow survives death has been going on for thousands of years, probably since man first realized that he does indeed die. Each age explains the search in terminology popular in its time. In the late eighteenth and early nineteenth centuries the popular terminology was that of animal magnetism.

While the stage mesmerist, the Svengali with the glowing eyes, remains a popular stereotype, even today, few realize how far down the road to out-and-out spiritualism many of the early magnetists went. Dr. Billot used to hold regular seances with his somnambules. The phenomena produced by the magnetized subjects were identical to that produced by spiritualist mediums a quarter century later. Wrote Billot of one experience:

"Towards the middle of the seance, one of the seeresses exclaimed 'There is a Dove—it is white as snow—it is flying about the room with something in its beak—it is a piece of paper. Let us pray.' A few moments later she added, 'See, it has let the paper drop at the feet of Madame J——.' "

When Billot picked up the paper packet he found that it exuded a sweet smell and contained three small pieces of bone glued onto small strips of paper, with the words "St.

Maxime," "St. Sabine," and "Many Martyrs" written beneath the fragments.

On another occasion one of the somnambules said that she saw a maiden holding out a branch covered with flowers. Suddenly one of the members of the seance party cried out that something had been dropped into her lap. It was a piece of Cretan thyme. Similar "apports" were regular features of spiritualist seances.

Nor was that all. Even the cautious Deleuze had heard things that he believed were beyond human understanding and perhaps dangerous. He wrote to Billot: "A great number of somnambulists have affirmed that they have conversed with spiritual intelligences and have been inspired and guided by them, but I will tell you why I have thought it best not to insist on such facts and proofs of spirit communication. It is because I have feared that it might excite the imagination, might trouble human reason and lead to dangerous consequences." He added tantalizingly, "I have suppressed many things in my works because I considered it was not yet time to disclose them."

Yet the experiments in France were tame when compared to the phenomena being produced by the magnetists in Germany. Probably the most famous German case of that era centered about Frau Frederica Hauffe, "the Seeress of Prevorst." In 1826 the seeress came under the care of Justinus Kerner, a poet, physician, and well-known magnetist. She was obviously a sick woman, for since birth she had suffered from convulsions, fallen into spontaneous trances and seen visions. Kerner first tried to alleviate her condition by various orthodox treatments, and when these failed he turned to the magnetic trance.

For the remaining three years of her life the seeress was

under Kerner's care. During this period she spent more time in a trance than out. While entranced she was able to diagnose other people's diseases, see distant events, trace the past and foresee the future. She also saw ghosts, and while in her presence Kerner occasionally saw them too:

"On the 8th December at seven in the evening," Kerner wrote, "I happened to be in Frau H.'s outer room, from which one could see into her bedroom. I saw there a cloudlike figure (a gray pillar of cloud as though with a head), without any definite outlines. I seized a light and hurried silently into the room with it. There I found her staring fixedly at the spot where I had seen the cloudy form. It had disappeared, however, from my view."

The seeress presence also seemed to be accompanied by poltergeist phenomena, objects moved mysteriously, stones were thrown at windows, and so forth.

Kerner was convinced that magnetism released extraordinary powers in the woman. After the seeress' death, he wrote a highly influential book concerning her accomplishments. Unfortunately, examining the phenomena the seeress seemed to produce, one disturbing fact crops up: except for the ghosts or whatever it was that Kerner himself saw, support for all the supernatural events depended entirely on the seeress' family, particularly her sister, who was the seeress' constant companion. Most of the instances of prophecy and clairvoyance were confirmed only by members of the Hauff family. The seeress' sister was present at all the physical manifestations, and was the sole witness to most of them. It is quite easy to see how all of these marvels were due not to animal magnetism, but to a conspiracy on the part of the Hauff family with the seeress herself as the witting or unwitting front.

Many of the seeress' visions concerning man's body, soul

and spirit, and the relationship of man to the immortal and nonmaterial universe were pretty standard mystical stuff of the day. Her unbelievably complex and detailed system of Sun-Circles and Life-Circles, which apparently had some relationship to spiritual conditions and the passage of time, was more original. Kerner recorded all these speculations with what has aptly been described as "amazing patience." After her death a cult of followers sought to expand and illuminate these revelations about circles. There must be a deep satisfaction in this sort of dogged numerological calculation, for it has been done often enough.

The Seeress of Prevorst claimed to use a primitive universal language which she said was the language actually spoken by the Biblical patriarchs. She often uttered words or sentences in this "language" and said that it was the common language of her inner life. The characters that she drew to illustrate the "language" look Hebrew but appear rather more complex. The possession of some sort of secret but ancient and universal language has also been a common claim of occultists for centuries. Today we still find individuals who say that they have discovered the key to the language spoken on the lost continent of Atlantis or Mu, "the Motherland of Man." Speaking in unknown languages or "speaking in tongues" was part of the early Christian church services and is still quite respectable in some denominations today.

While a few mystics still revere the memory of the Seeress of Prevorst, history has not been kind to her. Frank Podmore, a skeptical but sympathetic and careful recorder of paranormal phenomena, wrote, "We find in Frau Hauffe and her kind indications of systematic trickery, often of a puerile character, whose only object appears to have been the satisfaction of a diseased vanity, conjoined with trances and ecstasies apparently genuine and outpourings, also probably not less genuine, of religious feeling."

Though Mesmer's marvelous discovery is today used in such mundane activities as dentistry, the aura of the fantastic and the supernatural still clings to it. Anyone who wants to laugh at the nineteenth-century Germans who stood open-mouthed in admiration of the Seeress of Prevorst should also recall the incredible case of Bridey Murphy which burst upon the American public in 1956. Under hypnosis a young Denver housewife supposedly revealed her previous life as an eighteenth-century Irish colleen. The story was later exposed, not as a conscious hoax, but as an act of wildly misguided enthusiasm on the part of an untrained hypnotist, and some of those who publicized the story. The Bridey Murphy case took hold of the American imagination because a lot of people still believe—in a vague sort of way—that a hypnotized person is in some sort of state of superconsciousness, and moreover that a hypnotized person is incapable of telling anything but the truth.

CHAPTER VII

Daniel Dunglas Home

The last half of the nineteenth century was, without question, the golden age of the spirit medium. On stages, in princely palaces, in middle-class living rooms and the barren rooms of poverty-stricken farms the inhabitants of the spirit world seemed to be making themselves known through the agency of mediums. The spirits produced strange raps, caused tables to rock back and forth, and materialized ghostly hands and feet. Flowers and jewels showered down, apparently out of thin air. Exotic perfumes tantalized the nostrils, while strange and ghostly music assailed the ears. Spiritualism swept the United States and Europe like a religious revolution or an epidemic of irrationality, depending upon your point of view.

Foreshadowings of the coming spiritualist explosion could be seen in the visions of Swedenborg, "the higher phenomena" produced by the magnetists, and in the revelations of such seers as the American, Andrew Jackson Davis. The world was certainly ready for something like spiritualism. But the spark that set off the explosion was a rather unlikely one.

Spiritualism really began in the little town of Hydesville, New York, about thirty miles east of Rochester. Hydesville is in a region sometimes called the "Burned-Over District." It was said that this area had been burned over so many times by religious revivals that there were precious few souls left to be set aflame. The Shakers, the Millerites, the Perfectionists, and other apocalyptic sects all found the district fertile ground for making conversions. Joseph Smith, founder of Mormonism, had his first visions of the fringes of the Burned-Over District.

The reaction to the events at Hydesville proved that the area had been misnamed; there was plenty of combustible material left in the Burned-Over District. In March of 1848 strange noises were heard in the house of blacksmith John D. Fox. His two young daughters Kate and Maggie said that these thumps or raps were communications from the spirit of a peddler who had been murdered in the house, and that they could interpret the code sent from beyond the grave. Later an older married daughter, Mrs. Leah Fish, also began receiving similar spirit communications.

This spooky but simple event created an unbelievable amount of excitement. Within a few years the Fox sisters were international celebrities who appeared, in the pitchman's language, "before all the crowned heads of Europe."

Once more the cry was raised that the immortality of the soul had at last been scientifically proven, beyond the shadow of a doubt. This new technique of communicating with the dead gave rise to the movement called spiritualism. In practice there was little new in spiritualism. The phenomena of the spiritualist seance were in no way different than those produced by magnetic somnambulists in their seances, but the new spiritualist movement had a broader appeal. A mere six years after the Hydesville rappings began some fifteen thousand American spiritualists signed a petition to the Congress of the United States, requesting some sort of official recognition of their movement. Though there were spiritualists in Congress (and there probably still are), most congressmen took a rather lighthearted view of the subject. A senator suggested that the petition be referred to the Committee on Foreign Relations: "We may have occasion to enter into diplomatic relations with the spirits." Another suggested the Committee on Military Affairs. Amid laughter, the matter was tabled.

Not everyone in the country was laughing. The success, both financial and social, of the Fox sisters encouraged a whole host of imitators who produced even more startling manifestations from the spirits. One by one these mediums were exposed, either as sad, self-deluded individuals or simple tricksters, or a confusing combination of both. Maggie Fox herself confessed that the raps that made her world-famous had been produced by cracking her big toe. One newspaper commented that Maggie Fox had located "the origin of Modern Spiritualism in her great toe."

From this rather depressing and disreputable collection one truly extraordinary figure stands out—Daniel Dunglas Home. Home was well aware of his own superiority, and he furiously denounced most of the other mediums of his day: "When the last of the dark seance mediums has abandoned his or her vocation in order to set up as a third rate conjurer, and the last puppet-box, alias cabinet, is demolished . . . the golden day of our cause's triumph may be accounted at hand."

Home, like most other occultists, was deliberately vague about his background. Though he wrote an autobiography, he revealed little. Friends and relatives who wrote about him were equally unenlightening. Home was apparently born near Edinburgh, Scotland, in 1833. He never spoke of his mother and father, though in a footnote in one of his books he states that his father was the illegitimate son of Alexander, Tenth Earl of Home. If nothing else, D. D. Home was an active social climber.

More probably the medium himself was illegitimate, for at a very early age, he was adopted by a Mrs. Cook, his mother's sister. When he was about nine years old, Home was taken by his aunt to America. The distant connection with aristocracy that Home tried to establish seems like an afterthought. While in America young Daniel always signed his name Hume. Only when he returned to Britain did he begin to use the more aristocratic spelling of Home.

Young Daniel and his foster parents settled in Connecticut, where he could hardly have been unaware of the spiritualist fervor inspired by the Hydesville rappings. Daniel quickly became involved in spiritualist doings in his region. Soon the Cook household was invaded by strange knocks and mysteriously moving furniture. Mrs. Cook, a rigid Presbyterian, was not happy about the spirit manifestations under her own roof, so Daniel departed to stay with more sympathetic friends. He was then eighteen years old and forced to live by his wits, a task at which he succeeded admirably. Home began to give seances and word of his powers spread rapidly among spiritualists in the northeastern states.

Thus D. D. Home established a style of life which varied little over the next few decades. He moved from one person's house to another and only occasionally took a place of his own. He never accepted direct payment for his seances, but he graciously accepted offers of lavish hospitality and gifts, including sums of money, and later quantities of jewels.

Home's American odyssey lasted for five years and carried him through much of the Northeast. In 1855 a group of his friends set up a committee and raised money to send the medium to England, partly as a missionary for spiritualism and partly for his health. Home suffered from tuberculosis, and the spirits advised him to go to England for the sake of his lungs, which was probably the worst medical advice ever offered to anyone.

In England, as in America, Home stayed with wealthy friends and gave private seances, which were attended by some of the country's most eminent personages. But as autumn approached Home went to Italy, and spent the next several years on the Continent.

Shortly after his arrival in Italy two curious incidents took place. In December 1855 Home was walking through the streets of Florence at night when he said he was attacked by a man with a dagger, who seemed intent upon murder. Home said he fought off the attacker and escaped with only a slight flesh wound. The following spring, Home announced that his spirit guides warned him that he was about to lose his mediumistic powers. At about this point he became a convert to the Roman Catholic faith, had an audience with the Pope, and claimed he was on the point of joining a monastic order. This flirtation with Catholicism lasted less than a year. A summons from the Emperor Napoleon III and his superstitious wife, the Empress Eugénie, to hold a seance at the Tuileries seems to have restored Home's powers.

Among those who attended Home's seances at the Tuileries was the visiting Tsar of Russia. Home became acquainted with many Russians and in 1859 he dashed off to St. Petersburg to marry one. She was Alexandrina de Kroll, seventeen-year-old daughter of a noble Russian family and the possessor of a modest fortune. The great author Alexandre Dumas served as best man at the wedding and Tsar Alexander II blessed the bride and gave her a diamond ring.

Within three years, however, Home's young wife died from tuberculosis that she apparently caught from her husband. The medium was left with an infant son and in rather pinched financial straits. For the next few years Home eked out a living giving public lectures and recitations and by publishing his autobiography. During this period Home spent most of his time in London. When he made a trip to Rome to study sculpture he was expelled by the papal government for the practice of sorcery. Home was, by the way, a passable sculptor and some of his wealthy associates commissioned busts from him.

In 1866 a group of friends and admirers of Home got together and formed a society called the Spiritual Athenaeum. The main purpose of the group seems to have been to provide D. D. Home a regular income. He was given the salaried position of secretary of the Spiritual Athenaeum.

Shortly thereafter, Home became involved in what was to prove the most embarrassing episode of his career. He met a wealthy and childless widow, Mrs. Jane Lyon, aged 75. Under direction from the spirit of her dead husband (who was speaking through Mr. Home, naturally), Mrs. Lyon presented the medium "as a free gift" the princely sum of twenty-four thousand pounds. Within a few months she had transferred to him over sixty thousand pounds. In gratitude for all these "free gifts" Home changed his name to Home-Lyon. Mrs. Lyon had more or less "adopted" the medium. But the widow proved fickle and soon fell under the influence of another medium. She asked for her money back, but Home refused to give it to her, and in April 1868 the whole thing wound up in court.

A large number of prominent people testified to the genuineness of Home's powers and his high moral purpose, but the court was unimpressed. The Vice Chancellor stated, "As I hold spiritualism to be a delusion, I must necessarily hold the plaintiff to be the victim of a delusion."

Home was not specifically charged with fraud, or with tricking Mrs. Lyon into making the gifts, but the court was also not satisfied that Mrs. Lyon's gifts were, "acts of pure volition, uninfluenced." It was a fine distinction. Home was forced to return the money.

During the trial Home reported another of those mysterious attacks by a dagger-wielding assassin. This time the attack was supposed to have taken place on the stage of an empty London theater. Again there were no witnesses to the incident, and again the medium managed to escape with only a slight wound. The Lyon vs. Home trial had been pretty hilarious anyway, and this story simply added to the general merriment.

Home's loss in court hurt his pride but did not shake the faith of his spiritualist friends one iota. During the next few years Home was extremely active as a medium. It was during this period that he was reported to have performed some of his most remarkable feats in the seance room.

In the autumn of 1871 Home married another Russian heiress. He was received into the Russian Orthodox Church, and seems to have severed most of his connections with his former spiritualist friends, though both Home and his second wife remained vocal supporters of the spiritualist movement.

Home now spent most of his time in fashionable Auteuil, France. His health, which had never been robust, grew steadily worse. The nineteenth century's most celebrated medium died in 1886 in France. The immediate cause of death was pneumonia. He was fifty-three years old. Home was buried in the Russian cemetery at St. Germain-en-Laye under the inscription "To Another Discerning of Spirits."

This, in outline, is the life of Daniel Dunglas Home. From it one might conclude that Home was an adventurer, a soldier of fortune, and an international confidence man. He was undoubtedly all of these things, but he was a good deal more. The last half of the nineteenth century was not only the great age of mediums, it was also the great age of medium exposés. Every major medium of the time was thoroughly and publicly exposed as a fraud (though spiritualists usually refused to believe the exposures or excused them on the grounds that the same mediums also produced "genuine phenomena"). Every medium was exposed except D. D. Home. Home had numerous enemies inside spiritualist circles as well as among anti-spiritualists. They would have loved to catch him in the middle of a trick, but no one was ever able to pin anything conclusive on Home.

Though many of Home's admirers were both credulous and stupid, thus poor witnesses, the medium also captured the admiration of men of great learning and keen perception. Even some total disbelievers in spiritualist manifestations have come away from the case of D. D. Home suspecting that there was "something" beyond simple parlor magic that accounted for his enormous influence. We must look at the man and what he accomplished more closely.

When Home first entered the spiritualist scene he seems to have been a physically attractive young man. A contemporary described him thus: "He is but seventeen years old, tall for his age, fair complexion, hair neither red, brown, nor auburn, but a complete mixture of the three—like a three colored changeable silk—rather inclining to curl; and beautiful hair it is, as you can imagine; a large broad forehead, well developed, lively grey eyes, nose not remarkable, and a handsome mouth and teeth; easy manners, very intelligent for his age; perfectly artless and very affectionate."

Pictures of the mature Home show him as an ordinary, even a funny-looking fellow. A friend, but an objective one, Ian Perdicaris, described Home as "not good-looking, though his face was as a rule pleasant to look upon; very vain of his personal appearance, with a quite innocent and not unpleasing vanity. Always pleasing manners, very affectionate towards all—men, women, and children alike." In England, Home was occasionally criticized for his "barbarous American manners."

Beauty is, as always, in the eyes of the beholder. One reporter who attended a Home lecture in 1866 described him as "a slim, lithe gentleman, with pale face, light hair, and small dark eyes . . . with dainty white hands . . . The spirits could find no fault with the perfectly respectable appearance of their professional advocate." Another reporter who attended the very same lecture saw "a tall, thin, cadaverous man with long yellow hair. His hands long, white, and bony. When he shows his glittering, sharp teeth and that red rim comes round his slowly rolling eyes, he is not a pleasant sight to look upon."

An impressive list of literary and scientific figures were impressed with Home, among them were Elizabeth Barrett Browning, John Ruskin, Turgenev, Dumas, and the co-author of the theory of evolution, Alfred Russel Wallace. But Home had his prominent enemies, too. Thomas Henry Huxley regarded all spiritualism, and Home in particular, as fraudulent. The great Michael Farady experimented with various devices used by spiritualists and found all the results were explainable by natural means. Nor were all the literary figures of the age under Home's spell. Charles Dickens attacked

Home repeatedly in the magazine he edited. In a letter Dickens stated that even if the medium "were demonstrated as humbug in every microscopic cell of his skin and globule of his blood, the disciples would still believe and worship."

Home's angriest enemy was Robert Browning, who was incensed over his wife's infatuation with the medium. Browning composed a poetic attack on spiritualism called "Mr. Sludge the Medium." Home was the model for the cringing faker Mr. Sludge.

Some of Home's friends had a simple explanation for Browning's hatred of Home—they said he was jealous. In a seance attended by the Brownings, Home materialized a hand bearing a garland. Browning, they said, thought the garland was for him, but instead the spirit hand placed it on his wife's brow. This infuriated the poet, and provoked him into writing "Mr. Sludge."

Browning certainly thought that Home was a fraud. But Browning had seen fraudulent mediums before. This does not account for his genuine fury with Home. Another reason for Browning's hatred has been suggested by psychical researcher Eric J. Dingwall.

> . . . There was clearly something else that Browning knew about Home which excited him unduly. That something was, I suspect, the mystery of iniquity about which Lord Normanby's brother told Mrs. Browning three years later. What was this mystery? It was, I think, something that to-day we should take little notice of, but in those days was considered something very dreadful. Home was one of those individuals whose sexual inclinations were at times somewhat inverted. His friendships and dealings with young men were such as to arouse suspicion. His public life made all such stories assume a shape which had no justification in fact. My own view, for which there is now

considerable evidence, is that Home was homosexually inclined but rarely, if ever, allowed his inclinations any practical expression . . .

Dingwall believes that it was suspicion of homosexuality that caused the French police to hustle Home quickly and quietly out of France in 1857. Shortly before Home's visit to France there had been a major homosexual scandal in the French court.

Home's most faithful admirers had to admit that he was not a saint, that he was a vain, often selfish man who was ever on the lookout for the soft touch. Yet he conveyed an impression of utter sincerity about his mediumistic powers. During his trances, Home would often utter long rambling sermons that were "very touching and beautiful. A pure, lofty, and religious tone more or less pervades them," according to one of his admirers. Home's writings about the "mission" of spiritualism carry a message of vague but conventional morality. Both sermons and writings seemed to provide reassurance and comfort to those who believed them. The principal message was the truth of immortality.

While in a trance Home was said to deliver messages from dead friends and relatives of the sitters in his seances. Though these messages were not set down verbatum, many of those who received them were impressed by the amount of intimate detail they contained. Spiritualists contend that Home could not have known this information by ordinary means.

It is such "messages from the dead" that are the mainstay of most mediums today. But the last half of the nineteenth century was the era of physical mediumship. The spirits had to do a lot more than just talk; and when D. D. Home was around they did.

Here is an account of one of the more unusual and possibly

significant manifestations that took place at a Home seance during the medium's time in America. The account was written by R. T. Hallock, M.D., a leading spiritualist and concerns a seance held at the home of Charles Partridge, editor of the *Spiritual Telegraph*.

"On the table around which we were seated were loose papers, a lead pencil, two candles, and a glass of water. The table was used by the spirits in responding to our questions, and the first peculiarity we observed was that, however violently the table was moved, everything on it retained its position. When we had duly observed this, the table, which was mahogany and perfectly smooth, was elevated to an angle of thirty degrees and held there, with everything remaining on it as before. It was interesting to see a lead pencil retaining a position of perfect rest on a polished surface inclined at such an angle. It remained as if glued to the table and so of everything else on it. The table was repeatedly made to resume its ordinary position and then again its inclination as before, as if to fasten upon us the conviction that what we saw was no deception of the senses, but a veritable manifestation of spirit presence and of spirit power. They [the spirits] were then requested to elevate the table to the same angle as before and to detach the pencil, retaining everything else in their stationary positions. This was complied with. The table was elevated, the pencil rolled off, and everything else remained. They were then asked to repeat the experiment, retaining the pencil and everything else upon the table stationary except the glass tumbler and to let that slide off. This was also assented to with the like result. All the articles retained their positions but the tumbler, which slid off and was caught in the hands of one of the party as it fell from the lower edge of the table."

In a typical Home seance, bells, accordions, and other musical instruments were played mysteriously, spirit hands grasped people's trouser legs, and occasionally appeared above the table, spirit lights became visible, and the medium himself might float up to the ceiling according to witnesses. Home's seances usually took place in dimly lit but not entirely darkened rooms. A couple of candles or a single gaslight provided the only illumination, but compared to most seances where the mediums insisted on total darkness, Home's seances might be called well lighted. However, the "higher manifestations" of spirit power, like the levitation of the medium, took place only after the medium adjudged the conditions to be right. Then the candles were blown out, the fire screened, and these wonders occurred in almost total darkness.

Most of the manifestations that Home produced during his seances were common property among the mediums of his day. Home himself seems to have attracted no special attention while he was in America. It was only after he went to England and the Continent that his influence became predominant in spiritualist circles.

It was not that the manifestations of Home's seances became more spectacular (though he was able to produce a few effects that seemed beyond the powers of most other mediums) that accounted for his great success. Rather it seems that Home's success as a medium was due primarily to his ability to disassociate himself from other mediums, and from the world of professional spiritualism in general. Thus he removed himself socially from the fakers who were crashing down on all sides of him, and was not tainted by their exposure, at least in the eyes of his friends.

Though it was tremendously popular, spiritualism was in endless turmoil as each new mediumistic "star" was caught employing trickery. Even those most devoted to the cult could not help but feel that there was something distinctly unrespectable about mediums. Home moved rapidly to increase the social distance between himself and other mediums and to be identified solely with his rich and aristocratic patrons. In so doing he became almost as immune to suspicion of fraud as they were.

Home's conflict with the extraordinary Madame Blavatsky (H.P.B), founder of Theosophy, gives a clear indication of where the medium's sympathies lay. H.P.B. had abandoned a comfortable position in the Russian aristocracy to roam the world as an adventuress and free-lance occultist. Home, who had begun in poverty and obscurity and had married a Russian heiress, was moving in the other direction. A clash between these two gigantic egos was inevitable.

While holding a seance in America, H.P.B. claimed that a spirit had presented her with a military decoration taken directly from her father's grave. Home wrote a letter pointing out that H.P.B. had used exactly the same trick during a Paris seance some years earlier. He also noted that it was not customary to bury Russian military men with their decorations, as H.P.B. had claimed.

In one of the extravagant fantasies H.P.B. concocted to cover her own shady past she claimed that her illegitimate child was actually the child of a Baron Meyendorf by another woman. H.P.B. said she had merely kept the child to protect the Meyendorf name from scandal. In fact, though H.P.B. had known Meyendorf well, he was almost certainly not the child's father. Meyendorf also happened to be a good friend of Home's and Home was outraged by the story. He rose to the defense of his aristocratic friend, against his occultist colleague. Home rarely missed an opportunity to publicly ridicule H.P.B.'s theosophy. At one point H.P.B. proclaimed that Home was her chief tormentor and had driven her from America to India. In a lifetime of making enemies H.P.B. discovered that D. D. Home was one of the most formidable.

It was Home's total identification with his wealthy sitters—they were his friends, not his spectators, clients, or employers—that really accounts for his never having been exposed. Home was never publicly exposed because he never performed publicly. He had virtually complete control of the conditions under which he operated. Most mediums were forced to give public performances where anyone, including the unfriendly and the critical, could attend. They often had to submit to investigations of their powers by skeptical committees and individuals. Home never took these risks. When he appeared publicly it was as a lecturer for spiritualism, not a medium. Even when hard-pressed for funds he turned down attractive offers to give public seances.

A seance with D. D. Home tended to be a cozy little affair, much more of a gathering of friends, who in an atmosphere of mutual trust set out to explore the mysteries of the spirit world, than a test of the medium's power. Not all of those who met Home were impressed by his powers, but such skeptics, if they figured to become troublesome, could easily be excluded from a seance. Dr. E. Barthes, a physician at the court of Napoleon III in France, was one such skeptic. He tried to attend a Home seance in 1857, but the medium announced that there were too many people in the room and the doctor was asked to leave.

However, the doctor reported in a letter to his wife that another sitter had discovered the secret of some of Home's marvelous manifestations. "At the proper moment he [Home] throws off a slipper and with his naked toes tugs at a dress here and there, rings a handbell, gives a rap on this side or that, and then slips his foot back into his slipper again."

Another of Napoleon III's court circle, Viscount Beaumont-Vassy, commented in his memoirs, written years later, that under the table Home had presented his unshod foot to Napoleon as the spirit hand of Queen Hortense.

Home complained that such critics made out that he had the toes of an orangutan. But in fact, most mediums had been caught red-handed, or more accurately red-footed, ringing bells or producing other "spirit" manifestations with their toes. Professional magicians easily reproduced the most baffling spiritualistic phenomena, principally by using their feet.

Another protection Home had was that he made no promises about what would happen at a seance, so he was never put into the position of having to produce phenomena on demand. At many seances very little happened. Only when conditions were "right" would the more difficult and doubtless risky "higher manifestations" be attempted.

Thus Home held all the cards—he could do what he wanted, under conditions which suited him, and in front of an audience of his own choosing. Small wonder he was never exposed.

"Unfair!" those believers in psychic phenomena might cry. Home was investigated perhaps more closely than any other medium in the history of spiritualism. And the investigation was not carried out by "psychical researchers," whose objectivity is always in question, but rather by Sir William Crookes, one of England's foremost scientists.

Crookes remains a bone in the throat of every antipsychical skeptic. He was a man of undoubted learning, who had accomplished much in the fields of chemistry and physics. He became president of the famed Royal Society. Yet Crookes

Hermes Trismegistus

Faust raises the Devil.

The alchemist's laboratory. After the picture of Breughel the Elder, engraved by Cock (sixteenth century).

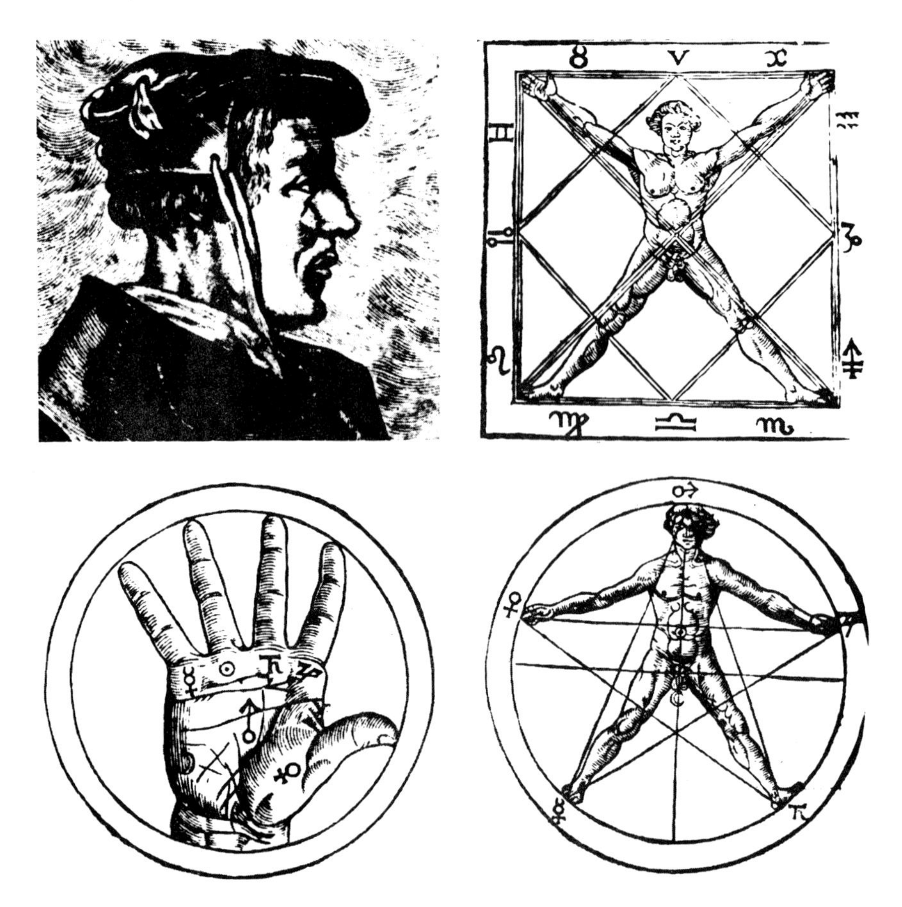

Cornelius Agrippa and some of the illustrations from a seventeenth-century English edition of his book on occult philosophy.

The Order of the Illuminati, a mythical group of occult masters. Among the members were supposed to be John Dee (lower left) and Edward Kelly (center right). Other members included Appollonius of Tyana, Roger Bacon, Mohammed, and Paracelsus.

Edward Kelly in the act of invoking the spirit of a deceased person.

OPPOSITE: *The fabulous mirror in which magicians were supposed to be able to see past, present, and future.*

F. A. Mesmer

Mesmer's celebrated baquet. *The iron rods radiating from the tub were supposed to direct the "magnetic rays."*

Emanuel Swedenborg

Maggie Fox

Kate Fox

Leah Fox

The spirit of Katie King appears in this highly imaginative picture of a Victorian seance in Philadelphia.

PHOTO COURTESY OF THE SOCIETY FOR PSYCHICAL RESEARCH

Daniel Dunglas Home

PHOTOS COURTESY OF THE SOCIETY FOR PSYCHICAL RESEARCH

Two pioneers of psychical research: William Hodgson and Sir William Crookes.

PHOTOS COURTESY OF THE SOCIETY FOR PSYCHICAL RESEARCH

Madame Blavatsky

Hodgson's diagram of occult room with the shrine at Adyar. From Proceedings of the Society for Psychical Research.

REFERENCE.

1. **Thinwall substituted for original window.**
2. Hole in wall behind the middle panel of Shrine.
3. Four-panelled boarding originally at back of recess immediately behind Shrine.
4. Bricked frame forming front of recess.
5. Aperture formed by removing bricks from one partition of the bricked frame.
6. Door of sideboard.
7. Hinged panel at back of sideboard.
8. Cupboard with secret double back opening into passage.

PHOTO BY ANGUS MCBEAN

Eileen Garrett

not only confirmed that D. D. Home seemed able to control some "new force," he went on to confirm the genuineness of other mediums, including the Fox sisters, who were admitted frauds. Far more spectacular than his investigation of D. D. Home was Crookes' later investigation of Florence Cook, an attractive young medium whose specialty was calling up the scantily clad form of Katie King, a popular spirit control who had been used by other mediums. Crookes confirmed that there was no fraud involved in Florence Cook's seances. Yet even the devout have had a hard time swallowing the "spirit" of Katie King.

In 1962 Trevor H. Hall, a British jurist and psychical researcher, re-examined the Crooke's-Cook case and came to the sensational conclusion not that Crookes had been fooled (as many had believed) but that he was an active participant in the hoax, and that he had a sexual involvement with the attractive medium. Though all the figures in this case were long dead, the charge stirred up a fantastic furor in the very tradition-minded psychical research circles in England. The controversy reverberates to this day. While Hall's theory is as plausible as it is sensational, there is no way of proving the charge, or of disproving it either, unless, of course, one summons up the spirits of Crookes, Cook, or Katie King. And if that could be done, the charge would be irrelevant.

True or not, Crookes' later deep involvement with spiritualism, while it may cast grave doubts on his accuracy as an observer, does not automatically discredit his experiments with Home.

The Crookes-Home experiment was undramatic enough, and fairly typical of early (and many modern) investigations of paranormal phenomena. Home was asked to change the weight of a piece of wood suspended from a spring balance.

What exactly this has to do with spirits and ghosts that make up the main attraction of paranormal phenomena is a little hard to see at first glance. It was assumed that the force that moved the balance was the same "spirit" force that tipped tables, rapped out messages, produced spirit hands and other materializations. Since no one had ever been able to measure this force it was also assumed to be nonmaterial. Once the existence of a nonmaterial force was proved, one could then postulate an entire nonmaterial or spiritual universe, and it seemed that this would finally provide the ironclad proof of the immortality of the human soul.

Crookes' equipment was quite elaborate for what should have been a rather simple experiment. His write-up of the experiment in the *Quarterly Journal of Science* of July 1871 is crammed with all sorts of information about the conditions of the test, including such minutiae as the temperature of the room and sort of wood used. At first glance this experiment with Home seems the very model of scientific precision and control, with all irrelevant factors screened out. A second look, however, shows that the structure of the experiment had holes in it easily large enough for an experienced medium like Home to crawl through. Crookes specifically did not screen out the possibility that Home might cheat.

While Home was supposed to be under observation at all times during the test, he was not. There were four observers in the room beside Crookes. At first nothing happened, and so Home was allowed to wander about as he pleased. The observers all had other duties to perform and could not have watched the medium closely.

Though Crookes recorded the temperature of the room, he said little about how the room was lit, and there are indications that the lighting was very dim. In other experiments

Home specifically asked that the lights be turned down. Still, when the moment came the "spirits" through the agency of D. D. Home seemed able to register about three pounds of extra weight on the balance, by apparently nonphysical means.

How did Home do it? According to Frank Podmore, the skeptical and thorough investigator of spiritualist phenomena, Home used the same method he used for keeping objects on tilted tables—he attached a black thread to them. Such a method is often used by stage magicians. In a dim light a dark thread is virtually invisible. On the tilting table, Home could have released threads selectively, so that first one and then another object would be allowed to slide. The trick was a risky one. Threads might get tangled, or someone might brush against them and ruin the illusion. Once Home left America it seems that the phenomenon of the stationary objects on the tilting table was rarely produced in his seances.

There would have been much less risk involved in using a thread in Crookes' laboratory. Only a single thread was needed and it could easily have been attached to the balance while Home wandered about the lab. If the other end of the thread were attached to the knee of his pants the medium could have exerted three pounds of pull on Crookes' balance by a barely perceptible bending of his leg.

Podmore, who had the highest respect for Crookes' honesty and intelligence, had this to say about him: "His previous training did not necessarily render him better qualified to deal with problems differing widely from those presented in the laboratory. To put it bluntly if Home was a conjurer, Mr. Crookes was probably in no better position for detecting the sleight-of-hand than any other man his equal in intelligence and native acuteness. Possibly even in a worse position; for it may be argued that his previous training would prepare the way for Home's efforts to concentrate attention on the mechanical apparatus, and thus divert it from the seemingly irrelevant movements by which it may be conjectured the conjurer's end was attained." Misdirection of attention is the number one weapon in the conjurer's bag of tricks.

The history of psychical research has often borne out Podmore's thesis, for scientists have been easily fooled by tricks that professional magicians detected at once. A professional magician has told me that he has found scientists among the easiest people to fool because they are so sure that they cannot be fooled.

Perhaps an even more basic problem with the investigation was that neither Crookes nor anyone else whom Home allowed to "investigate" his powers could truly regard the medium as a trickster. Home got no money for the tests, yet he freely gave of his time. He seemed to be fully cooperative, and as anxious to find out what strange powers he possessed as were the investigators themselves. Home was charming, and highly respected by intelligent and socially prominent people. He was, in short, a gentleman, and not the sort of man who would resort to cheap tricks. None of the sitters at Home's seances would have thought of grabbing the "spirit hand" to see if it really were the medium's foot, though they had doubtless heard rumors that it was. In the same way Crookes and his fellow investigators would not have been so impolite as to tell Home to sit down and stop messing about with the equipment, nor would they have ordered him stripped and searched in the middle of the experiment. Remember that Home operated in Victorian England. In this polite and formalized society to have openly doubted the word of a gentleman like Home would have been intolerably impolite. It was simply assumed that everyone was acting in good faith. Besides, if Home thought he faced exposure he could simply have broken off the experiment claiming that the influences were unfavorable.

At this late date there is, of course, no way of proving that Home fooled around with Crookes' weighing apparatus. But the fact that he could easily have done so makes Crookes' tests less than conclusive.

The spirit hands, the rappings, the apports, musical sounds, spirit voices, and the like were the most common features of Home's seances. But such phenomena were also the common property of practically all the other nineteenth-century mediums. These phenomena have so often been proved to have been produced by ordinary legerdemain that all but the most credulous believers in psychical phenomena have difficulty in taking them seriously, even in the great Home's seances. But Home was able to produce a few effects that were not common coin among the mediums of his day, and are still highly regarded by those with an interest in psychic phenomena.

First there were the "elongations"—Home's apparent ability to grow taller right before the very eyes of his sitters. Again it is a bit difficult to imagine just exactly what this ability had to do with contacting the spirit world, but a few other mediums attempted similar elongations. Any unusual ability shown by the medium was—illogically in my view—looked upon as proof of his supernatural powers in all areas. The elongation feat was doubtless impressive, and buttressed the belief that Home possessed powers beyond those of ordinary mortals.

As usual this feat was performed only in front of a group of Home's special friends and few made any attempt to carefully record or analyze what they had seen. But one of Home's aristocratic associates, Lord Lindsay, wrote this account in 1869 for the London Dialectical Society, which was investigating spiritualism:

"On another occasion I saw Mr. Home, in a trance, elongated eleven inches. I measured him standing up against the wall, and marked the place; not being satisfied with that, I put him in the middle of the room and placed a candle in front of him, so as to throw a shadow on the wall, which I also marked. When he awoke I measured him again in his natural size, both directly and by the shadow, and the results were equal. I can swear that he was not off the ground or standing on tiptoe, and I had full view of his feet, and moreover, a gentleman present had one of his feet placed over Home's insteps, one hand on his shoulder, and the other on his side where the false ribs come near the hip-bone."

When Lord Lindsay was questioned later about Home's feat, he explained:

"The top of the hip-bone and the short ribs separate. In Home they were unusually close together. There was no separation of the vertebrae of the spine; nor were the elongations at all like those resulting from expanding the chest with air; the shoulders did not move. Home looked as if he was pulled up by the neck; the muscles seemed in a state of tension. He stood firmly upright in the middle of the room, and before the elongation commenced I placed my foot on his instep. I will swear he never moved his heels from the ground. When Home was elongated against the wall, Lord Adare placed his foot on Home's instep, and I marked the place on the wall. I once saw him elongated horizontally on the ground; Lord Adare was present. Home seemed to grow at both ends, and pushed myself and Adare away."

Some have suspected Home of having concealed telescoping

stilts in his pants' legs to perform his elongations, but it seems doubtful that Home would have used such a crude and clumsy device, and he would not have needed it.

We can all stretch a little bit if we try, and a supple person with practice can stretch to an astonishing degree. Milburn Christopher cites the case of "an honest showman" named Clarence E. Williams, who toured the vaudeville circuits some sixty years ago as "The Man Who Grows." Writes Christopher: "Surrounded by a committee from the audience, the five-foot-nine-and-a-half-inch marvel would zoom up, inch by inch, until he towered high above the men who stood near him. In his prime Willard could add eight inches to his height, though newspaper critics who wrote about his act said he grew a foot or more." Willard also performed his specialty in hospitals under careful medical supervision.

Christopher described seeing Willard, then an old man, lecture before a session of the Society of American Magicians. Though the veteran performer was over eighty at the time he still managed to "grow" five inches during his talk.

Willard never laid claim to any supernatural powers. He said he had merely trained himself by constant stretching. He got his idea for the performance by watching tigers at the zoo stretching for exercise.

Now if we grant that Home produced some of his seance marvels by trickery, we must also accept that he was an accomplished conjurer, and as such an agile individual, for agility is necessary in sleight-of-hand illusions. We can see that Home could have produced his marvelous "elongations" simply by stretching like Willard had. This is no small accomplishment, but it is no indication of supernatural powers. Home need not have been nearly as proficient as the showman either. While Willard performed on stages before critical, if not downright hostile audiences, and under careful medical supervision, Home gave his performances only in darkened seance rooms, and in front of groups of friends and admirers. As already pointed out, such witnesses, while not necessarily dishonest, would not be the most acute observers, for they already believed deeply in Home's powers. Such witnesses could easily and honestly have exaggerated, in their own imaginations, a stretching of a few inches into an elongation of a foot or more.

By beginning in a relaxed stance, with knees slightly flexed, Home could have "grown" a couple of inches simply by straightening up. Though Lord Lindsay says that a foot was placed firmly on the instep of Home's shoe, was the light in the room good enough for him to be sure that the medium's foot was actually fully inside of the shoe? Perhaps the medium slipped partially out of his shoes and stood on his tiptoes while the shoe itself was flat on the ground. If Home's shoes had a reinforced instep they would not have changed shape when he slipped out of them, and the man with his foot on the instep of the shoe might never have known.

Exactly how Home worked this trick we can no longer say. Probably he had several alternate techniques, depending on the circumstances. Most conjurers do. But it is clearly unnecessary to invoke the spirits to explain this one of Home's manifestations.

Another feat performed by Home that was largely unknown among lesser mediums was the "fire ordeal." On rare occasions during seances, the medium would walk over to the fireplace and pick up a glowing coal in his bare hands. Crookes was a witness to two of these fire ordeals and was much impressed by what he saw.

"At Mr. Home's request, whilst he was entranced, I went

with him to the fireplace in the back drawing room. He said, 'We want you to notice particularly what Dan is doing.' [While in a trance Home always referred to himself in the third person as Dan.] Accordingly I stood close to the fire and stooped down to it, when he put his hands in. He very deliberately pulled the lumps of hot coal off, one at a time with his right hand, and touched one which was bright red. He then said, 'the power is not strong on Dan's hand, as we have been influencing the handkerchief most. It is more difficult to influence an inanimate body like that than living flesh, so as the circumstances were favourable, we thought we would show you that we could prevent a red-hot coal from burning a handkerchief. We will now collect more power on the handkerchief and repeat it before you. Now!'

"Mr. Home then waved the handkerchief about in the air two or three times, held it above his head, and then folded it up and laid it on his hand like a cushion; putting his other hand into the fire he took out a large lump of cinder red-hot at the lower part and placed the red part on the handkerchief. Under ordinary circumstances it would have been in a blaze. In about half a minute he took it off the handkerchief with his hand, saying, 'As the power is not strong, if we leave the coal longer it will burn.' He then put it on his hand and brought it to the table in the front room, where all but myself had remained seated."

On another occasion Crookes reported:

"Mr. Home again went to the fire, and after stirring the hot coal about with his hand, took out a red-hot piece nearly as big as an orange and putting it on his right hand, covered it over with his left hand, so as to almost completely enclose it, and then blew into the small furnace thus extemporised until the lump of charcoal was nearly white-hot, and then drew my attention to the lambent flame which was flickering over the coal and licking round his fingers; he fell on his knees, looked up in a reverent manner, held up the coal in front, and said, 'Is not God good? Are not His laws wonderful?' "

On some occasions Home seemed able to stick his head into the fire without singeing a hair. At other times Home walked around the room carrying a glowing lump of coal. Those who believed implicitly in the medium's powers were allowed to handle the glowing coal, and were not burned. They reported that the coal only felt "warm." According to one woman Home put a glowing coal on her head and drew her hair up around it. She reported feeling only a sensation of warmth. Those who hesitated, drew back, or in any other way showed that they had less than perfect confidence in Home were not allowed to touch the coal. Home would mutter, "Little Faith —Little Faith," and pull the coal away, claiming that they would be burned if they touched it. Some said that they reached out anyway and actually had been burned.

Home's "fire ordeal" must have looked pretty sensational in the Victorian world. Today, however, it seems less so, even to those who believe in Home's powers. We have all seen or at least heard about circus "fire eaters." We have also heard about the fire walkers of Fiji and other places. The whole phenomena of fire walking and of fire eating have been examined quite closely. There are several secrets to success in handling fiery objects, but none of them have anything to do with the supernatural.

First, some "red-hot" or "white-hot" objects are not nearly as hot as they appear to be. The pits of hot rocks or glowing ash across which the fire walkers tred are carefully prepared, and while they look very hot, the surface temperature is not so high that the flesh will be seared upon contact.

One stage medium who practiced the "fire ordeal" would regularly appear to thrust her face into the flames. Yet she refused to hold her thumb briefly over an open flame. Her performance was broken up in a riot by the enraged customers.

A second factor in handling hot objects is confidence and speed. Fire walkers move very rapidly once they have stepped into the fiery pit. They make no missteps, and no one becomes frozen with fear as you or I might. If they did they would become severely burned. Stage performers also know just how to handle fiery materials, how long they can be safely held, etc.

An unknown psychological factor is faith and suggestibility. A person who really believes that he will not be burnt is less likely to feel pain than a person who is quite sure that he will be hurt. Of course, the man who grasps the heated end of a red-hot poker is going to be burned, faith or not. But in marginal cases, where an object is not overpoweringly hot, a man who thinks he cannot be burned may report the object as simply being warm, while another man will feel that the same object has burned him, and may actually develop blisters from the contact.

Clearly Home himself regarded the entire fire ordeal as a dangerous feat, either because he might be burned, or because the trick might be exposed. He showed it only under unusually favorable circumstances, to a small but select group. If Home actually did walk around with a red-hot coal, as he was described as doing, then he was able to do something far beyond the skills of an ordinary performer. But how accurate were the descriptions? This feat was always performed in nearly total darkness and at the end of a long and emotionally exhausting seance. The sitters had already been treated to many "marvels" and were in a highly suggestible state. Was Home really picking out one of the hot coals at random, or was he employing some sort of illusion? Christopher notes that a charred piece of white pine, introduced among the burning coals in a fireplace, may be handled with ease.

The ultimate D. D. Home feat was levitation. Home wasn't the only man in history reputed to possess the power of levitation. Many ancient magicians, and some saints, St. Francis and St. Theresa among them, were said to occasionally be raised above the ground by some supernatural power. Many mediums regularly performed "levitations" during seances. The illusion of floating is almost astonishingly easy to create in a dark room. Levitation was one of the "higher manifestations" Home reserved for the final and darkest part of his seances.

The medium has one of the sitters grasp the toes of his shoes, which are held close together. Then the medium just slips out of his shoes, grabs them in his hand and raises them into the air. To the man holding the shoes it seems as if the medium's feet are rising off the ground. If the medium then stands on a chair he can raise the shoes to great height, creating the illusion that his feet were very near the ceiling. With the shoes on his hands the medium might touch the sitters on the forehead with his heels. The shod hands held horizontally and passed quickly in front of a dimly illuminated window might actually create the illusion of the feet of a man floating above the ground. All of this time, of course, the medium keeps talking about how he is being carried into the air and is floating about. The suggestible sitter will then begin to believe that he has actually seen what he has only been told.

It is hard to believe that such a crude and obvious trick could work among a group of people who were not complete idiots, yet it can and does. Professional magicians have repeated the illusion and fooled intelligent and observant people with it. Professional mediums have also confessed that this is how they performed their levitations.

While most of Home's levitations were performed in darkness or near-darkness the ubiquitous Crookes says that he saw Home levitated in enough light to get a clear view. One report of a Home levitation in America that took place in full light is simply a rumor that has never been tracked down.

A fairly typical Home levitation is described in this account:

"Shortly after this a very curious affair took place . . . Mr. Home remarked, 'I feel as if I am going to rise.' The room was quite dark. He said, 'I am getting up,' and as I was only a few feet from him I put out my hand to him. I indubitably felt the soles of both his boots some three feet above the level of the floor. On my doing so he said, 'Don't touch me, or I shall come down.' Of course, I instantly desisted, but down he came. In less than five minutes after this he remarked, 'I am again ascending,' and from the sound of his voice we could not but infer that he was actually rising towards the ceiling of the ante-room."

At another seance, witnesses reported seeing the medium's feet and legs floating horizontally near a window.

Both of these manifestations can easily be ascribed to the old shoes-on-the-hands trick. But as usual Home did his contemporaries one better, and performed a couple of levitations that have become classics in the annals of parapsychology.

The most famous of these levitations, and probably the most celebrated single mediumistic feat in modern history took place on December 16, 1868, on the fourth floor of Ashley House on Victoria Street in London. (There is a great deal of dispute over where this particular seance took place.) Beside Home three other men were present in the darkened seance room, Lord Adare, Home's good friend and close companion; Lord Lindsay, another frequent sitter at Home's seances (they were the two witnesses to the elongations mentioned earlier); and Captain Charles Bradstreet Wynne, Adare's cousin.

What happened in and out of Ashley House that night has been a matter of great controversy for a century. To read modern spiritualists one would get the impression that the three witnesses saw Home actually float out of his chair, into the next room, out through a window, and back in through the window of the original room. This is not what was reported. Though one may doubt that the three witnesses were the most competent observers no one has ever doubted their honesty. They honestly attempted to report the incident as they saw it.

Several months after the event Lord Adare wrote: "We heard Home go into the next room, heard the window thrown up, and presently Home appeared standing upright outside our window; he opened the window and walked in quite coolly."

In a fuller account Lord Lindsay mentions seeing Home's shadow going out horizontally through the window of the next room, and seeing the shadow of Home's feet hovering some six inches above the window sill, and hanging there for a few seconds before Home stepped to the sill and entered the room.

The third witness, Wynne, in general confirmed the story that had been related by the other two. These accounts were not written down for some months after the incident, and they contain a few minor discrepancies, but they should not be brushed aside, for they appear essentially accurate. What then happened?

The shadows of the floating feet are easy enough to explain. Home probably did go out through the window horizontally, and he may have balanced himself rigidly on the window sill to create the illusion of floating. We know Home was capable of this because shortly after the levitation the medium gave Lord Adare a striking demonstration. Adare commented that the window through which Home was supposed to have floated was not open very wide and he was surprised that the medium had been able to get through it at all. Home asked Adare to step back and then "went through the open space, head first, quite rapidly, his body being nearly horizontal and apparently rigid." Home's hands were outside the window and Adare could not see whether he was holding on or not. We may assume that he was. Balancing rigidly on a window sill would have been easily within the physical abilities of a man as supple as Home. Thus, even if someone had been impolite enough to look into the other room when Home was supposed to have been floating out through the window, it would have looked as if he were.

There is some confusion as to whether Home appeared outside the window of the room in which the witnesses were sitting in a horizontal position or standing upright. Lord Adare is most definite on the subject. He says, "Home appeared standing upright outside our window." The shadow of floating feet that Lord Lindsay saw could easily have been produced by the medium's holding onto the molding on top of the window so as to suspend his feet off the sill for a few seconds.

Thus, in this most famous of all mediumistic levitations, no one actually saw Home float anywhere, and no one said that they did. They simply assumed that he *must* have floated. The only question that remains is how Home got from one window to the next. According to Lord Lindsay, "the distance between the windows was about seven feet six inches, and there was not the slightest foothold between them, nor was there more than a twelve-inch projection to each window, which served as a ledge to put flowers on." The drop to the pavement below was some eighty feet.

Houdini suggested that Home could have hung a wire outside of the window, on which he could have swung from one window to the next. The rooms and the building were well known to Home, and the medium himself had suggested both the time and place for the seance. He had plenty of opportunity to string up a wire, or a more elaborate apparatus if he had wished. Trevor Hall, who re-examined the evidence on the case, concluded that Home could actually have stepped from one window to the next. (According to one contemporary account of the event the seance was held on the first floor.)

When Home rejoined his companions after his reputed levitation he was chuckling to himself. "We are thinking," he said in his customary third-person manner of talking about himself, "what if a policeman had been passing and had looked up and seen a man turning round and round along the wall in the air he would have been much astonished." No doubt! But if that policeman had been passing by we might have a better idea of just exactly how the medium accomplished this particular feat. As it is, we may still entertain a strong suspicion, one bordering on certainty that Home got from one window to the next by perfectly ordinary means.

This illusion seems so childishly simple that there is a great temptation on the part of critics to denounce the three witnesses to the "levitation" and to all the other Home marvels as a pack of credulous fools. This sort of denunciation is unfair both to the witnesses and to Home. It also assumes that intelligent and observant men cannot be fooled—they can, and have been, and will be again.

Many of the witnesses at Home's seances gave a pretty accurate description of what they saw. They tended to explain what they saw by invoking the supernatural, rather than by looking for the trick. Most of the sitters at Home's seances accepted the reality, or at least the possibility of supernatural powers. They liked Home and trusted him. Many also may have entertained the illusion that only a fool can be easily fooled.

In this famous levitation seance the witnesses gave better reports than one might expect, given man's rather imperfect powers of observation. But Home was no ordinary creator of illusions. During the levitation he did not simply pretend to float out a window; if he had, his friends might have been unconvinced. Rather, he carefully prepared the minds of the witnesses for what was supposed to happen. A few days before the seance two of the sitters saw Home standing on the ledge of the very window through which he was later supposed to float. The sight of Home on the ledge terrified Lord Lindsay, who thought the medium was about to fall. During the seance, Lord Lindsay thought he saw a ghostly apparition, and just before the levitation itself, spirit voices told the sitters what was about to happen.

Home undoubtedly possessed extraordinary powers of suggestion. Podmore, who disbelieved the claims of all mediums to produce any supernatural physical manifestations, postulated that most of the habitués of Home's seances were extraordinarily suggestible individuals, and that Home himself seems to have possessed some power of causing hallucinations. He concluded his discussion of Home with this: "There is, then, some evidence for the view that a medium's equipment may include a faculty of inducing false perception in his clients."

I am reminded of the old radio show *The Shadow,* where the hero had "the power to cloud men's minds." Perhaps D. D. Home had some of that power too.

One final question. Did Home believe any of the spiritualist business that he practiced with such superb skill? No confession of trickery survives, nor did he ever seem to boast of his tricks to an intemperate associate, as so many mediums have done. If Home used confederates, they were as close-mouthed as he. Within the tight circle of Home's friends and family there would have been a natural tendency to hush up any loose talk about the master. But there is no hard evidence that anything damaging was ever suppressed, and Home's many enemies have worked hard to discredit him.

Obviously no one can work the fancy tricks that Home did without being quite aware of what he is doing. Yet it is still possible that some of Home's moralizing, either while apparently entranced, or in his lectures and writings, may have been quite sincere. He might have believed, as others have suspected, that his power over people was not entirely a natural human attribute. And he may really have had moments in which he believed he was in touch with the invisible world. I find it difficult to imagine that a complete cynic could have concealed his feelings so well for so many years.

CHAPTER VIII

Madame Blavatsky

HELENA PETROVNA BLAVATSKY may well have been the most brilliant and audacious charlatan who ever lived. She lied, connived, and bullied her way through life on four continents. She shamelessly used and misused her most devoted friends, and was responsible for at least one suicide and innumerable ruined lives. After leading a dissipated youth, she demanded strict asceticism from those who surrounded her. No one who was ever closely associated with her can truthfully be said to have come out the better for it, except for those who learned her tricks and used them to their own advantage.

Yet, now that she has safely been dead for eighty years, one cannot help but express almost unbounded admiration for "the Old Lady." While the cautious D. D. Home was never exposed, H.P.B., as she usually signed herself, was exposed almost constantly, by skeptics, rivals, disillusioned followers, defecting confederates, and she herself engaged in periodic public confessions of one sort or another. She possessed an uncanny knack for picking associates as untrustworthy as herself, and had an addiction to cheap and obvious tricks that even the credulous had trouble swallowing. Yet the exposures never humbled her for more than a moment. Rather, they seemed to inspire her to more outrageous and fantastic efforts. The warnings of hordes of disillusioned followers did nothing to stem the flow of new converts to her cause, and often the disillusioned themselves joined up for another dose, and another, and another.

H.P.B. was a great rebel, and she gloried in this. As she wrote to her biographer: "I am repeatedly reminded of the fact that, as a public character, as a woman who, instead of pursuing her womanly duties, sleeping with her husband, breeding children, wiping their noses, minding her kitchen and consoling herself with matrimonial assistants on the sly and behind her husband's back, I have chosen a path that has led me to notoriety and fame; and that therefore I had to expect all that befell me."

H.P.B. was in no way an ordinary woman of her time, or of any other time. The things she really did are very nearly as fantastic as the things she claimed she did.

While many occultists, and others, have manufactured bogus noble backgrounds for themselves, H.P.B. had to do no such thing. Her father, Peter Hahn, was a Russian officer and a descendant of petty nobility. Her mother, Helena Fadeev, was quite well born, and could trace her family back to a ninth-century grand duke.

Helena was born on August 12, 1831, at Ekaterinoslav in the Ukraine. Her father, Captain Hahn, was off to the wars in Poland and his young wife had been sent to the home of her maternal grandparents to have her baby. After the Polish campaign, the Captain's wife and infant daughter joined him in southern Russia, where he was stationed.

Life in an army garrison is never easy for wives and children, and the conditions which prevailed in the Russian army of the 1830s were almost unbelievably barbarous. Helena's mother was an intelligent and sensitive woman who could not abide the rough army life. She used every pretext to make extended trips to St. Petersburg. She also wrote some dozen novels from which she gained a limited measure of critical acclaim. All of these novels expressed Madame Hahn's disillusionment with men and with the society in which she lived.

Helena's mother was an extraordinary woman, and though she died when her daughter was only twelve, one can guess that her independent and cynical ideas had a tremendous influence. But H.P.B. steadfastly denied this. Later she tried to juggle dates so as to practically eliminate her mother from her life entirely. H.P.B. rarely mentioned her mother except to claim that Madame Hahn had died while she was a baby. It is not unreasonable to suspect that mother and daughter did not get on well.

"Lolo," as young Helena was nicknamed, was described as a sickly, hysterical, and wildly imaginative child. In these respects, at least, she changed hardly at all for the rest of her life. Though her mother moved in the sophisticated and enlightened circles of St. Petersburg, Lolo spent most of her time in the care of superstitious peasant nurses or in her father's army camp among the equally superstitious soldiers. She was filled with terrifying tales of goblins and evil spirits, which she used in turn to terrify her companions. Quite early the girl learned that her ability to construct fantastic tales gave her great power over others.

After his wife's death, Captain Hahn decided that an army camp was no place to bring up children. Lolo was put under the care of her maternal grandparents, the Fadeevs. General Fadeev was an important civil servant, and his wife was a remarkably well educated and intelligent woman who made real contributions to the study of botany. But the testimony for Madame Fadeev's abilities has to come from others beside H.P.B. She never credited anyone but herself with ability, and she would certainly never admit that anyone—of this world at least—had any influence upon her. Also from the testimony of others it was clear that the dramatic, self-centered, impulsive, half-mad, yet crafty qualities that marked her later life had become established quite early.

At the age of sixteen Helena was jilted by Prince Alexander Galitsin. Her hysterical reaction included, among other things, plunging her leg into boiling water in order to avoid attending a ball without him, and marrying General Nikifor Blavatsky on the rebound.

Later in life, when she played the role of ascetic saint, H.P.B. tried to prove that she was still a virgin and implied that General Blavatsky had been a man of seventy or eighty when she married him, and clearly much too old for any sexual activity. "Old" Blavatsky was in fact less than forty at the time and in excellent health. Ultimately he outlived his wife.

Though Helena bore the name Blavatsky for the rest of her life, the marriage itself was a farce and lasted only three months. Helena then stole a horse and fled back to her grandfather's house. The situation may have been an embarrassing one for General Blavatsky, but he made no strenuous attempts to get Helena back, and was probably quite relieved to get rid of the willful and wildly unpredictable girl. General Fadeev was not at all glad to have the escaped bride back in his house. Blavatsky was an old friend, and harboring the runaway would look bad. So General Fadeev attempted to ship her back to her father. Colonel Hahn traveled two thousand miles from St. Petersburg to Odessa to pick up Helena. Shortly before he arrived Helena slipped away from the servants who were watching her and sailed for Constantinople as the companion of the skipper of an English bark.

The year was 1848. Helena was then seventeen years old. For the next twenty-five years—until she appeared in New York in 1873—Helena wandered the world, having, one must assume, all manner of exciting and scandalous adventures. She was, after all, a young woman traveling alone, she had no known means of support, she was high-spirited, and at least for the first years of her travels passably attractive. Even after she had grown fat and ugly she never lost her power to attract men. But we have only the foggiest idea of where she went and what she did during this quarter century.

Later in life, as she attempted to put on the mantle of sainthood, H.P.B. had somehow to cover up what had occurred during the twenty-five years of wandering. She told so many different and often conflicting stories that the mind reels. But this was her technique for explaining embarrassing situations. She made the explanations so complicated and confusing that one tended to accept them from sheer weariness. She buried the uncomfortable facts in a soothing flow of ambiguous words. Other occultists have used the same technique, but few had quite so much to cover as she, and none were as imaginative. Her disciples have muddied the waters still further until there is not a single undisputed date or event during this period of her life.

But one can be reasonably certain about some dates and places. In about 1850 Helena was in Cairo, where she met a wealthy young American traveler named Albert Leighton

Rawson. Helena was then passing herself off as a widow, and Rawson found her charming. He recalled that she "could fascinate the most indifferent man in a single interview." They spent some months together and Rawson paid for Helena's lessons with a famous Coptic magician. Whether she was truly attempting to learn occult secrets or just trying to learn a few conjuring tricks is impossible to say.

Rawson also noted that at about this time Helena began using hashish. He reported that when he met her in New York some quarter of a century later she was still using the drug. The connection between drugs and occultism is a strong one, and it is a connection which polite dabblers in occultism often wish to overlook.

Perhaps even before she went to Cairo, Helena had met Agardi Metrovitch, a Hungarian operatic singer, and a wanderer himself. Although Helena often derided "old" General Blavatsky, Metrovitch was even older. Yet he remained Helena's off-and-on companion and perhaps her husband for the bulk of her wandering years. Explaining away the presence of Metrovitch proved to be one of Helena's most difficult tasks. Usually she did not mention him at all. Some of her followers tried to banish his name from all the records of her life. But occasionally Helena did have to account for Metrovitch and she was ingenious in doing so. At one point she said that Metrovitch had been sent by her family to find her in Cairo. But he was being pursued by Maltese gangsters who had been hired by the Pope to kill him because of his violently anti-Catholic activities. Helena, being warned through supernatural means of the plot, took Metrovitch into her house and would not allow him to leave.

Back in Russia a host of rumors about Helena (she was a circus bareback rider in Constantinople; working in Paris with D. D. Home, etc.) and occasional letters from different men (including Metrovitch), who introduced themselves as Helena's husbands, arrived at the Fadeev household. Late in 1858 Helena herself turned up. One of those who saw her during this return was her cousin Count Sergei Witte. Later he was to become one of Russia's most important and intelligent statesmen. Witte, who had heard all the delicious rumors about Helena, was greatly disappointed by her appearance. Though only thirty she had already gotten quite fat and her face "bore all the traces of a tempestuous and passionate life." Worst of all, she was incredibly sloppy and spent most of the day lounging about in a dirty old wrapper rolling cigarettes and swearing. Yet he had to admit that she possessed a certain fascination, and the most hypnotic and beautiful eyes that he had ever seen.

The Fadeev family was far from happy to have this prodigal return, and they tried their best to keep her out of sight. But it was no use. Helena soon became a favorite among the younger people by holding seances and showing off all the tricks that she had learned in Cairo, Paris, and Lord knows where else. Witte was astounded that so many intelligent people could be taken in by what seemed to him obvious sleight-of-hand tricks.

Helena was apparently struck with a momentary yearning for respectability, and she went to Tiflis where General Blavatsky was living in an attempt to patch up her marriage. Astonishingly enough General Blavatsky seemed willing to have her back, though he had not seen her in ten years. This reconciliation did not last much longer than the original marriage. Metrovitch turned up in Tiflis and Helena departed with him in a cloud of scandal.

When H.P.B. tried to pose as an ascetic she went to great

and largely unsuccessful lengths to prove that she was a virgin. Thus the birth of her child in 1861 became the single most difficult incident in her life to explain away. Even at the time, the child was extremely inconvenient. Helena didn't really have a husband, though in the eyes of the law she may have had several of them. The child's father was almost certainly Metrovitch. Early in 1861 Helena headed south to the remote Russian border provinces of the Trans-Caucasus. She bought a house in Ozoorgetty in the province of Mingrelia, an unlikely place, but it was a Russian army outpost and thus she had the services of an army physician. At this point, according to the stories she later told, Helena fell ill and remained in a semiconscious state for the next few months. There is no mention of the birth of a child. Yet after the Ozoorgetty interlude, Helena had a small child named Youry with her.

H.P.B.'s later attempts to account for the presence of the child descend into deliberate incoherence. The idea that she could be the child's mother is not even mentioned. But she does indicate that the child's father was Baron Nicholas Meyendorf, a young nobleman who was much attracted by the occult and was a regular habitué of spiritualist circles. That the Baron had at one point been Helena's lover there can be little doubt. He admitted it, and his family did apparently pay Helena some money to keep her quiet. But it is very doubtful if the child was his. The charge not only infuriated Meyendorf, but also enraged his good friend D. D. Home, and touched off the fierce quarrel between H.P.B. and the celebrated medium.

As a matter of fact, Metrovitch acknowledged being the child's father, though later H.P.B. claimed that he did this only to protect the Baron's good name. The child, Youry, was continually referred to as "crippled," "sickly," or "unfortunate" and he did not survive beyond the age of six. During Youry's brief life, Helena, Metrovitch, and the boy lived mostly in Italy. If she felt any sadness over her child's death H.P.B. never expressed it publicly.

While the child had been alive Helena's life seems to have been relatively tranquil—at least there was little traveling. But after his death, she and Metrovitch took to the road again, this time back to Russia. There they once again encountered Witte, who described the couple as "a toothless lion, perennially at the feet of his mistress, an aged lady, stout and slovenly." (Helena was then forty, hardly aged but doubtless both stout and slovenly.) Helena hatched numerous money-making schemes, all of which ended in failure.

In 1871 the couple again left Russia aboard the S.S. *Eumonia,* but off the coast of Egypt the ship either was wrecked or exploded, and most of the four hundred passengers died. Metrovitch was among them. Witte said that he died saving Helena, but she never mentioned this. Indeed, in later years she said Metrovitch had been poisoned a year earlier by agents of the Pope.

The future did not look very bright for Helena. She was abandoned in Egypt without a penny to her name, and no family or friends willing to help her. She had lost her looks, and the only skill she possessed was a tolerable mastery of parlor magic. But Helena Petrovna Blavatsky was nothing if not resilient and resourceful.

Cairo in the 1870s was haven for a shabby and disreputable army of spiritualist mediums. Helena was forced to join this group, but in order to raise herself above the common run of Cairo mediums she formed what she called the *Société Spirite,* and advertised her grandiose claims in the spiritualist press of

Europe. The *Société Spirite* didn't last long. One day a patron found a cotton-stuffed glove hanging from a string behind the cloth lining of a wall. The glove was pulled out during seances to represent a spirit hand. H.P.B. quite naturally denied having anything to do with the fake and blamed it all on another medium who shared the premises. Members of the *Société Spirite* were not satisfied with the explanation. There was a small riot and Madame departed hastily from Cairo.

Later that year she turned up in Russia once again. Although she always loved Russia above any other country, H.P.B. could never bear its restrictive atmosphere for long. Within a year she was off again, this time to Paris. Rumors of unspecified but scandalous behavior surrounded her Paris stay. A few months later she decided to cut all ties with the past and start a new life in a new land. With virtually no funds at all she embarked for New York in June 1873.

At that time immigrants by the millions were pouring into the United States. H.P.B. first found lodging in a philanthropic home for working women on New York's Lower East Side. She even tried working, making artificial flowers in a sweatshop. But H.P.B. was no ordinary immigrant, and she struggled mightily to keep herself from being swept along with the anonymous millions. She quickly established contact with spiritualists, other Russian immigrants, newspapermen, in short anyone who might be able to help her out of her dismal situation. Her father died at about this time and a few hundred dollars of inheritance helped ease her plight momentarily. But H.P.B. was no manager of money and the inheritance was soon gone. She needed a major break.

The break came when Madame spied a series of articles in the New York *Graphic* concerning the remarkable mediumistic phenomena that were being produced at the farm of the

Eddy brothers in Vermont. The articles were written by Colonel Henry S. Olcott, a newspaperman, lawyer, and an ardent spiritualist. During the Civil War, Olcott had gained some reputation for exposing fraud and corruption in army arsenals. This success had earned him the rank of colonel. The Colonel, however, proved much less than skillful at exposing mediumistic frauds. He wrote glowing reports about the Eddy brothers' tawdry tricks. Olcott was an upright and honest man, though not overbright, and his sincere will to believe often caused him to see some things that were not there and ignore some things that were. Even at this stage in his career it is clear that Olcott was more than willing to turn a blind eye to obvious frauds if he thought it would help the cause of spiritualism.

The manifestations at the Eddy farm were quite ordinary, and Olcott was having trouble keeping up the interest of the public. But after H.P.B. arrived on the scene the excitement picked up considerably. Previously the spirit guides had been an uninspiring pair of Indians named Santum or Honto and the squaw Bright Star. With H.P.B.'s arrival the spirits became more international in character. There was a Kurdish warrior, a black African, a Hindu, a Georgian peasant (the spirit of a former servant in the Madame's household), and a host of other figures who seemed even more exciting and exotic in rural Vermont.

But it was not to see the spirits or to produce them that had tempted H.P.B. to travel to the Eddy farm. In the hard months which had preceded her visit to Vermont she had furiously schemed and plotted ways by which she could be propelled to the lucrative forefront of the American spiritualist world. Time was running out and H.P.B. knew it. She had spent a quarter of a century roaming the world, and now past forty she was still penniless and still obscure. If she was to "make it" in the world she had to do it soon. Upon reading Olcott's articles, H.P.B. decided that here was a man who could help her to a brighter future. As noted, H.P.B. possessed a genius for picking untrustworthy associates, but her choice of Henry S. Olcott was a stroke of great good fortune—for her, if not for Olcott.

Once at the Eddy farm, Madame concentrated all her formidable powers of fascination on Olcott. She flattered him, dazzled him with stories of her adventures (most of them untrue, for though she had many adventures they were not the sort that Olcott would have wished to hear about). She swore profusely, displayed a ferocious temper, smoked constantly (and this is an age when smoking was considered an infallible sign of an immoral woman), but Olcott was charmed. Within two weeks he was ready to believe anything she said.

After her return from Vermont, H.P.B. moved into an apartment across the street from Olcott's club, and through his influence she began mingling with the uppercrust of the American spiritualist world.

She also started a personal publicity campaign, and found that for her publicity was easy to come by. She was a character of the sort that delighted newspapermen of the 1870s, just as they do today. Her size and extreme sloppiness would have made her stand out in any crowd, and when she was arrayed in fancy dress in order to make an impression her appearance was grotesquely fantastic. Olcott tried to be as kind as possible in this description: "A stout and remarkable looking woman wearing a perky hat with plumes, a grand toilette satin dress with much trimming, a long heavy gold chain about her neck attached to a blue enamelled watch with a monogram in cheap diamonds, and on her lovely hands a dozen or fifteen rings, large and small . . . I have gone to the theatre with her when I expected the house to rise to us."

Madame invaded newspaper offices and treated bemused reporters to long, rambling interviews, which were reported tongue-in-cheek. Colonel Olcott, who was trying to make spiritualism more respectable, was distressed by such interviews. Madame, however, was not worried. She subscribed to the philosophy of, "I don't care what you say about me, so long as you spell my name right"—which didn't always happen either. In one article the name came out Blowtskey.

Eighteen seventy-five was a very important year in H.P.B.'s career. Perhaps the least important event of that year was that she married again, though she had never been legally divorced from General Blavatsky. This troubled her not at all. Her new husband was a young Russian immigrant named George Betanelly. A few months earlier Betanelly, who was at the time supposed to be completely unknown to H.P.B., had confirmed some of her revelations about Russia after supposedly reading about them in the newspapers. Olcott was much impressed by Betanelly's testimony, though if he had considered the matter closely, he would have discovered that the young Russian confirmed the printed stories before he could possibly have read them.

Just what drove H.P.B. to marry Betanelly is not at all clear. He seems to have been a rather simple fellow with no money and no prospects. Madame tried to pass the hat among her friends to get her young husband established in some sort of business, but the plan got nowhere. Soon she tired of Betanelly, and his mere presence upset her. She took to her bed with an attack of paralysis which was either completely feigned or psychosomatic. When one doctor suggested that her leg should be amputated she cured herself in a few days.

Then she sent Betanelly away on a trip, and finally after four months of marriage she went off to join Olcott, who was in Boston. She never saw Betanelly again.

Eighteen seventy-five, however, was a bad year for American spiritualism. A number of fraudulent mediums (many of whom H.P.B. had personally endorsed) had been thoroughly exposed. Their tricks were so gross that even convinced spiritualists were getting nervous. For the early months of the year H.P.B. fought fiercely to save spiritualism's declining reputation, but it seemed hopeless. "I am ready to sell my soul for spiritualism," she wrote to a Russian spiritualist, "but nobody will buy, and I am living from hand to mouth." She felt she must transfer her allegiance to a new occult movement, but which one? Finding none available, she invented one.

On March 9, 1875, Colonel Olcott received a glazed black envelope sealed with red wax. Inside, written in gold ink on thick green stationery was this letter:

> From the Brotherhood of Luxor, Section of Vth to Henry S. Olcott.
> Brother Neophyte, we greet Thee.
> He who seeks us finds us. TRY. Rest thy mind—banish all foul doubt. We keep watch over our faithful soldiers. Sister Helen is a valiant, trustworthy servant. Open thy spirit to conviction, have faith and she will lead thee to the Golden Gate of truth. She neither fears sword nor fire but her soul is sensitive to dishonor and she hath reason to mistrust the future. Our good brother "John" hath verily acted rashly but he meant well. Son of the world, if thou does hear them both, TRY . . . Thou hast many good mediums around thee, don't give up thy club. TRY. Brother John hath brought three of our masters to look at thee after the seance. Thy noble exertions

on behalf of our cause now give us the right of letting thee know who they were:

Serapis Bey (Ellora Section)
Polydorus Isurenus (Section of Solomon)
Robert More (Section of Zoroaster)

Sister Helen will explain thee the meaning of the Star and colors.

Activity and Silence as to the present.

By order of the grand
Observatory of Luxor. TUITIT BEY
Tuesday morning,
Day of Mars

The entire letter with its exotic names, colored inks, fancy symbols, and pseudo-archaic language sounds like something out of the cheap melodramatic fiction of the day. In tone it was. But there is nothing the confirmed occultist loves more than to be told that he is about to be let in on the mysteries of an ancient and secret mystic brotherhood. Today one can find active cults of flying saucer devotees who receive messages from the SI's (Space Intelligences), who are just the Brotherhood of Luxor brought up to date. Olcott was credulous, but he was no moron. Yet so strong was his will to believe and so powerful was H.P.B.'s influence that he swallowed the Tuitit Bey letter whole. In the years to come thousands were to be just as taken in by equally silly missives.

Letters from other worlds were nothing new. The "John" referred to in the Tuitit Bey letter was John King, the spirit father of the celebrated spirit control Kate King. For over a year the Kings had been sending, through the agency of Madame Blavatsky, letters to Olcott and other spiritualists.

While the Tuitit Bey letter was doubtless just a momentary inspiration, it served Madame's purpose admirably.

Olcott had been getting a bit restive about Betanelly, and the letter urged him to "have faith." It also implored him not to give up "thy club." This was the Miracle Club, a faltering spiritualist organization which Madame had hoped would support her. Though the spirit John was mentioned with the Brotherhood of Luxor, an entirely new concept had been born, and it paved the way for Madame to get out of ordinary spiritualism entirely, and ultimately to turn fiercely against it. The Brotherhood of Luxor itself was not destined for a long life. Soon these Egyptian adepts were replaced by a much more mysterious and awesome group, the Masters or the Mahatmas who dwelt in the wild mountains of Tibet.

H.P.B.'s great invention, theosophy, was born, at least in name, in that eventful year of 1875. Though spiritualism was in big trouble, and Olcott's Miracle Club wasn't getting off the ground, interest in occult mysteries was as strong as ever. Madame, Olcott and a few friends would often gather to hear speakers on different occult subjects. One night they heard a speech on the mysteries of ancient Egypt. The speech may well have inspired the Brotherhood of Luxor idea. Olcott was particularly intrigued, and wondered if a group could be formed to study such subjects. The old Miracle Club name seemed rather cheap. One of the members of the Blavatsky circle, Charles Sotheran, leafed through an unabridged dictionary and came up with the word theosophy. No one knew exactly what it meant, but it had the right tone, and so the first incarnation of the Theosophical Society was formed. Sotheran, who was well educated, skeptical, and highly independent, soon fell away from the group. H.P.B. could never tolerate independence. But it was Sotheran who gave her a new direction after her break with spiritualism and supplied many of the ideas that were incorporated into theosophy.

With the infant Theosophical Society just getting underway, H.P.B. embarked upon an ambitious new project. She was going to write a book. Again the idea was not original. At this time another medium, Emma Hardinge Britten, had published a popular book called *Art Magic*. Mrs. Britten insisted that she had not "written" the book herself, but that she had merely transcribed it under the direction of an invisible adept. Automatic writing under spirit control was an old device of mediums. That the writing had been directed, not by a spirit, but by some sort of remote mystic master, was an exciting new wrinkle. Many of the ideas in Mrs. Britten's book, the existence of an ancient occult science and of adepts who had mastered it, fascination with elemental races of the earth, etc., were similar to those espoused by the new Theosophical Society. This is hardly surprising, since in the wake of the debacle of organized spiritualism many of these ideas had been discussed by disillusioned spiritualists who were still seeking some sort of occult guidance.

Once launched upon a book project, H.P.B. was a prodigious worker. She often sat at her desk scribbling furiously from dawn till darkness, and for weeks on end she would not go out of her house. In fact, she hated to go out at any time. Any exertion more physical than eating, writing, or smoking was disagreeable to her.

Madame was as undisciplined in writing as she was in everything else. Olcott and another theosophist had to work mightily just to get her vast and unruly manuscript in shape for the printers. Even so, it took two years before the book titled *Isis Unveiled* could be published, and it had to come out in two volumes. Though the book strongly criticized much of spiritualism, particularly D. D. Home, the spiritualist press itself kept a respectful distance. The book was formidably large and the spiritualists didn't really understand it. They feared that it might just contain occult dynamite and that if they poked at it it would explode in their faces. The general press was much less respectful, and *Isis Unveiled* was derided as a great disorderly, plagiarized mess. Which is exactly what it is. *The New York Times* refused to review the book because the editors feared a flow of violently abusive letters from H.P.B. if the review was a bad one. But the occult-minded public loved *Iisis Unveiled.* The first edition of this virtually unreadable book sold out in ten days. It is still selling today.

While *Isis Unveiled* was being written, H.P.B. and Olcott finally began to live together openly. Olcott was married and had two grown sons. Though he and his wife had little enough to do with one another for several years, this open break with the respectability of the day marked a further submission of his will to H.P.B.

The couple moved into an apartment on Forty-seventh Street and Eighth Avenue. Olcott's newspaper friends nicknamed it the Lamasery. It was soon loaded with heavy Victorian furniture, Oriental curios, and a collection of international oddballs. The library of the Lamasery became one of the most celebrated and certainly the strangest salon in New York City, and perhaps in the entire world. Some of the projects hatched in the Lamasery were bizarre even by H.P.B.'s generous standards. One example will have to suffice.

A more or less permanent guest at the Lamasery was a shabby nobleman named Baron de Palm. He had led H.P.B. and Olcott on by tales of the great riches he was going to leave the Theosophical Society when he died. When the Baron unexpectedly did die, Olcott opened his luggage but could find only some of his own shirts, which the Baron had stolen. So they had this body, and no one knew quite what to do with it. Olcott, who among other things was interested in promoting cremation, decided that the Baron should be given a splendid public cremation. Services would be held in the Masonic Temple on Sixth Avenue and the body would be carried to a crematorium in Washington, Pennsylvania.

Though the Masonic Temple was the largest hall available, it wasn't big enough to handle the crowds, which nearly overwhelmed police reserves. Olcott led the procession, wearing a leopard skin, and other members of the Theosophical Society, dressed in pseudo-ancient Egyptian garb, followed along. Years later, Olcott recalled the silly incident with great affection.

With her new fame, H.P.B. found that her lurid past kept catching up with her and interfering with the image that she was now trying to project. She defended herself against the accusations—many of them true—in a variety of ways. One of her favorite weapons was to exaggerate the charges, then ridicule her own exaggerations. In 1877 she wrote a long letter to the New York *Graphic* complaining of "slanderous reports, vile insinuations, innuendo . . ."

". . . No retreat is secure against the anonymous slanderer who uses the United States mail. Letters have been received by my trusted friends containing the foulest aspersions upon myself. At various times I have been charged with (1) drunkenness; (2) forgery; (3) being a Russian spy; (4) with being an anti-Russian spy; (5) with being no Russian at all, but a French adventuress; (6) of having been in jail for theft; (7) of being the mistress of a Polish count in Union Square; (8) with murdering seven husbands; (9) with bigamy; (10) of being the mistress of Colonel Olcott; (11) also of an acrobat. Other things might be mentioned but decency forbids. . . .

"I hereby give notice that if any more unverifiable slanders can be traced to responsible sources I will invoke the protection of the law, which, on the theory of your national Constitution, was made for heathen [H.P.B. was violently anti-Christian, and always called herself a heathen] as well as Christian denizens. And I further notify slanderers of a speculative turn that no blackmail is paid at 392 West Forty-seventh Street."

Although some of the charges, like the one about murdering seven husbands, were obvious exaggerations, others like being a bigamist and a forger most certainly were not. Even the number of seven husbands may not have been too far wrong. H.P.B. would have been much better off simply ignoring the charges rather than putting them into the newspapers, even if it was to deny them. But discretion was never one of her strong points. She faced every challenge by rushing at it full force and hoping that she could overwhelm it by sheer audacity. Often that is exactly what happened.

During H.P.B.'s two-year absorption in the creation of *Isis Unveiled* the infant Theosophical Society had languished and virtually died. Olcott sadly reported that meetings had been canceled, and no dues could be collected. The resources of America itself seemed exhausted as far as H.P.B. was concerned, and she could not return to Europe, for she was too well known there already. Home's ferocious attacks upon theosophy had just been published and H.P.B. knew she would find no welcome among the spiritualists now. In 1877 she threatened to go to Australia, but that was not to be. Rather, she turned her eyes to the reputed home of all occult wisdom, the Orient, and particularly India.

Interest in Oriental religion and philosophy was increasing among occultists of the day. H.P.B. had included a good deal of it in *Isis Unveiled.* Among those who passed through the Lamasery were men who had traveled extensively in India, and they had put H.P.B. and Olcott into contact with some prominent Indians. But in the end the decision to depart for India was characteristically harebrained.

H.P.B., however, did show some foresight. Relations between Russia and England were strained, and England controlled India. She correctly foresaw that she might be accused of being a Russian spy, and might actually be denied entry to India. So as soon as she was eligible, H.P.B. became an American citizen. If there was one thing in the world that Madame loved—aside from herself—it was Russia. Thus, she found the whole business of becoming an American citizen thoroughly distasteful, but she did it and immediately prepared to leave.

Naturally Olcott, as second-in-command of the Theosophical Society, was going to make the trip, though he had grave misgivings. He had already cut his ties with his wife, but the thought of leaving his native land, perhaps forever, and never seeing his children again pained him greatly. And what would India be like? How would they live? It had been difficult enough to scrape together the funds to pay for the trip. (In fact, to this day there is some mystery as to where the money for the Indian venture came from. Some suspect that the Baron de Palm might have left a small legacy after all.) H.P.B. was always restless. She had spent her life wandering, but Olcott, though he held some strange ideas, was basically a conventional and rather cautious man. That he had agreed to make the trip at all is some measure of the totality of his surrender to Madame's more powerful will. To strengthen his resolve, the Brotherhood of Luxor bombarded the Colonel with messages confirming the wisdom of H.P.B.'s decision, and telling him of the great things that awaited in India.

When Olcott finally did reach India he fell to the ground to kiss the soil of the homeland of the "Mother of Mysteries." Madame was somewhat less emotional upon her arrival. But I believe that it would be wrong to think that she approached India in a completely cynical frame of mind. Though she had spent a lifetime bamboozling convinced occultists, H.P.B. was almost certainly a believer herself. At least, she really suspected that somewhere in the world there were adepts who possessed magical secrets that gave them great powers. Madame also believed that some of these adepts lived in India. During the early days of her Indian sojourn she went to great lengths to seek out such men in an attempt to pry their secrets from them, just as over a quarter of a century earlier she had attempted to learn the secrets of an Egyptian magician. Meanwhile, without having yet learned to produce real miracles, she continued to manufacture false ones to keep her followers loyal.

The Founders or the Theosophy Twins, as H.P.B. and Olcott were sometimes called, had expected a fairly enthusiastic reception in India. In their correspondence with Indians, the Founders had expressed a warm interest in the Hindu religion. The Indians, among them well-known scholars and religious leaders, had responded with almost touching gratitude. Once in India, however, the Founders discovered that they had misread the attitudes of their Hindu correspondents. Since India was a British colony it was customary for Indians to respond to all white men, British or not, with elaborate courtesy, but it meant little. Even the Indian who was to secure lodgings and otherwise prepare for the Founders' arrival in India proved to be a great disappointment. In his letters the fellow had sounded like a worshipful disciple of theosophy, so Olcott was shocked to discover that he had been grossly overcharging them and pocketing the difference. In truth, the fellow considered himself to be an employee, and was merely taking his pay in kickbacks, a time-honored custom in India and elsewhere.

The first few months in India were a time of depression and near panic, particularly for Olcott. He declared that the entire Indian adventure had been the "act of lunatics." As he saw their limited resources melting away, he warned that they would soon starve. H.P.B. was also depressed, but her entire life had been a succession of such uncertainties. Her greatest task was to keep Olcott from collapsing. This she did by showering him with letters and postcards from the Egyptian brothers, all urging him to persevere and assuring him that he was on the right track.

One might imagine that the most natural group upon which H.P.B. could exercise her strange charm would be the isolated and bored members of the British Civil Service in India. There would seem to be little profit in attempting to teach Oriental religion to Hindus. But with her characteristic audacity H.P.B. managed to anger the British right off. She openly declared her distaste for Christianity and praised the superiority of the Hindu religion. Many of the British were deeply offended. The Christian missionaries became her bitterest enemies. The police began to suspect that she really was a Russian spy out to disrupt British rule in India, and had her followed everywhere. Olcott protested to the government, and H.P.B. would stop on the street to scream abuse at her police shadows, but to no avail.

For her Theosophical Society in India, H.P.B. proposed rules that absolutely forbade racial discrimination, a totally unique idea in the India of that day. H.P.B. herself was without prejudice, or perhaps it might be more fairly said that she scorned all people equally. Of course, the great mass of poverty-stricken Indians held no interest for her. She concentrated on the small class of wealthy Indians, and among them she became surprisingly popular. She soon surrounded herself with a court of worshipful chelas, or disciples. Some of them seem to have been genuine converts to H.P.B.'s cause, while others were simply paid confederates.

Even the reserve of the British colonials began to crack under H.P.B.'s frontal assault. After a while some of them decided to take a closer look at this odd woman and see what she could do. They were shocked by her slovenly appearance, outrageous manners, and vile language. Her most important convert of this period, A. P. Sinett, wrote that she used words "that we should all have preferred her not to make use of." But H.P.B. did amaze some of the British with a succession of parlor tricks that she passed off as miracles.

Occasionally she attempted a fairly ambitious miracle. Once, while on a picnic with Sinett and some friends, the party discovered that there were only six cups and saucers—for seven people. A crisis at tea time! H.P.B. pointed to a certain spot in the ground and instructed one member of the party, a Major Henderson of the Indian police, to dig at that spot. There the Major dug up a cup and saucer of the same pattern as the set of six. Everyone was amazed and delighted. Major Henderson then went and examined the spot more closely and found indications that the china had been placed there by some agency other than a supernatural one. He asked H.P.B. to repeat the phenomena, but she threw a fit and accused everyone of doubting her word. Still the story of the mysterious cup and saucer was repeated around the clubs and drawing rooms of the English and not all of them heard the disappointing sequel. Even if they did there was no proof that H.P.B. or one of her confederates had actually buried the china. One could choose whatever explanation for the phenomenon one wished. Many chose to believe that a genuine miracle had been performed.

At one point Sinett asked H.P.B. for a conclusive test. Her adepts were supposed to have the ability to travel instantly from one place to another. He suggested that one of them should bring a copy of the *Times* of London to Bombay on the day it was published. This was a physical impossibility in the 1870s by normal means. H.P.B. indignantly turned down the test. The adepts could do this if they wished to, she said, but they would engage in no vulgar miracle-mongering. The test was too conclusive. It would convince everyone, and the masses who were not yet ready for enlightenment would be clamoring for it. One sees modern occults rejecting conclusive tests for much the same reasons.

It was a characteristic of H.P.B. and of many occultists to surround themselves with a wide variety of dubious miracles. If there are enough of them the devout seeker of wonders will conclude that not all of the phenomena could possibly be false. H.P.B. always operated on the theory that a dozen shoddy "miracles" were just as good as a single carefully prepared one. The devoted occultist is also ever hopeful that the next "miracle" will be the conclusive one, the one to silence all skeptics.

Once on the soil of India, the old Egyptian Brotherhood seemed somehow to lack the right tone. Gradually it gave way to H.P.B.'s greatest creation—the Masters or the Mahatmas. These were a group of adepts, mostly with Indian names, who were supposed to dwell in the remote and mysterious mountains of Tibet. With their ability to travel instantly from place to place, H.P.B. reported many direct meetings with them, and even her followers reported occasionally seeing one or more of the Mahatmas in the flesh. The Mahatmas usually turned out to be one of H.P.B.'s servants suitably garbed or some sort of dummy. In person the Mahatmas rarely spoke. They were just glimpsed running across a lawn or ducking behind a bush. When they wished to communicate they did so by letter, and their production of mail (or rather H.P.B.'s production in their name) was prodigious. At the height of their influence in the early 1880s the Mahatmas were turning out hundreds of thousands of words a year. Most of these letters were signed with the name of Master Koot Hoomi. The name was probably Madame's little joke, for it sounds as though it was made up of the names Olcott and Hume—at the time one of theosophy's more intelligent converts. The Mahatmas received letters as well as sent them through sort of an astral post office.

The "post office" arrangement was simple and efficient. If anyone wished to send a letter to the Mahatmas, they either gave it to H.P.B. or to her trusted chela and confederate Damodar. The Mahatma letters arrived in a variety of ways. Some came by ordinary mail. Others were delivered by H.P.B. or Damodar, still others appeared under pillows, fluttered down from ceilings, turned up under tea cups, etc. None of this was particularly difficult to arrange. It wasn't even new. H.P.B. and others had used all these tricks before. From the very beginning everyone, even those devoted to her, suspected that H.P.B. herself had written the letters. Yet they could not bring themselves to reject the attractive concept of the Mahatmas. The usual explanation offered was that H.P.B. had written the letters under the direction of the Mahatmas.

H.P.B. used the Mahatma letters as she had used the letters of the Brotherhood of Luxor, and John King: to get people to do what she wanted them to. She had the Mahatmas praise her friends and flay her enemies. They suggested projects that H.P.B. felt unable to suggest herself. The purpose of many of these letters was laughably transparent. Since H.P.B. was so mercurial, her "all-knowing" mouthpieces were sometimes forced to reverse themselves. Occasionally about-faces were so sharp as to be acutely embarrassing. One of the more embarrassing episodes concerned Swami Dayanand, a respected Indian religious teacher and reformer. The Swami had been sympathetic toward theosophy at first. He believed the theosophists to be a group of westerners sincerely interested in the Hindu religion, and in the fate of India. The Swami was H.P.B.'s biggest catch, and the Mahatmas praised him lavishly, even indicating that he might be one of them. But the Swami was quickly disillusioned, and began publicly denouncing theosophy as a fraud, and H.P.B. herself as an immoral adventuress. What to do? How could the Mahatmas have been so wrong about this man? In general they remained silent, or spoke in obscure phrases about the Swami's defection.

In another case, two of Madame's leading English converts had become dissatisfied with the way she was running things. So they decided to write directly to the Mahatmas and complain. But how could they deliver the letter? Since the astral post office worked only through Madame they had to give their letter of complaint to her. They simply could not believe that she would read mail addressed to the Mahatmas themselves. Yet just a few minutes after she was given the letter H.P.B. burst in upon them in an almost maniacal rage. Obviously she had just read the letter criticizing her. Yet only one of these disciples, both intelligent men, was disillusioned enough by the incident to abandon theosophy.

So powerful was H.P.B.'s ability to create a fantasy and have others share it that many clung to a belief in the reality of the Mahatmas long after they were convinced that Madame herself was a fraud. Such believers often wondered out loud why the Mahatmas associated with that strange and untrustworthy woman!

As with everything else H.P.B. did, the Mahatma letters appeared, from a distance, to be a crude and obvious trick. The Mahatmas, however, became more than mere mouthpieces for H.P.B.'s immediate schemes. Among the millions of words written in their name there are some really spectacular flights of mystical fancy, that rank among the best ever written. The speculations about the archaic history and cosmic future of mankind are mind-boggling. They more than equal the visions of genuine mystics like Swedenborg.

Most of all, H.P.B., through the Mahatma letters, was able to convey the soothing and comforting message which I think is at the heart of the appeal of most great occultists. The Mahatmas were a distant and all-powerful group, yet one which was concerned with the most intimate and apparently trivial activities of the little group of theosophists over whom they watched. It made everyone feel important. Inherent in H.P.B.'s rather disorderly scheme of the universe was the concept of reincarnation, so no one ever really need fear death. Finally, those who received the letters were given the feeling that their training, or period of testing, was moving along satisfactorily, and that very soon great secrets would be revealed to them. Something important was always just about to happen. This sort of anticipation can keep an occultist coming back for years, and serves as a powerful antidote to disillusionment.

The Mahatma letters also occasionally contained some

genuinely noble sentiments. Take this quote from the most mysterious and august Mahatma of them all, Maha Chohan himself:

"The Theosophical Society was chosen as the corner-stone, the foundation of the future religions of humanity. To achieve the proposed object a more benevolent intermingling of the high and the low, of the Alpha and Omega of Society, was determined upon. The white race must be the first to stretch out the hand of fellowship to the dark nations, to call the poor despised 'nigger' brother. This prospect may not smile to all, but he is not Theosophist who objects to this principle."

The suggestion is condescending, of course, but considering the time and place that these words were written the sentiments are really quite remarkable.

As usual, H.P.B. overplayed her hand, and she was giving her new critics in India larger targets to shoot at. Besides, there were disputes within the inner circle of theosophy. Her relations with Olcott had cooled considerably, and the Colonel now spent much of his time traveling, mainly in Ceylon and other distant places to spread the gospel of the Theosophical Society. Olcott was an effective public speaker, while H.P.B. was good only in small groups. The acclaim that Olcott began to receive on his trips gave him the courage to doubt H.P.B. and even to stand up to her a bit. The travels to Ceylon attracted Olcott and ultimately H.P.B. herself toward Buddhism, for they had never been comfortable with the multi-god universe of the Hindus. This disappointed many of theosophy's more devout Hindu followers.

When facing hostility, cult leaders often attempt to physically isolate themselves and their followers from the outside world. H.P.B. succumbed at least slightly to that urge. Financially theosophy was now a going concern. Through it, Madame controlled the resources of a fairly wealthy woman. She contrived to buy a large estate, which was actually more of a village or compound, in Adyar in the state of Madras all the way across India from her previous Bombay headquarters. Here she planned to live in peace with her devoted chelas, and entertain visiting theosophical notables from around the world.

As the *pièce de résistance* of this theosophical wonderland, H.P.B. conceived "the Shrine," the holy of holies, where miracles would be performed daily. At this point H.P.B. could probably have relaxed a bit and relied more on metaphysical philosophy than miracles to hold her followers. But, for all her success, and she had after all risen in ten years from a slum on the Lower East Side of New York to an estate in India, she could never rise above the cheap tricks of her early days as a medium.

To build all the sliding panels and secret doors that the Shrine would require, H.P.B. enlisted the aid of her associate M. Coulomb. Of all the untrustworthy individuals that she surrounded herself with, the two Coulombs were ultimately to cause H.P.B. the most trouble, and she certainly should have known it. Madame Coulomb had been an associate of H.P.B.'s during her early days as a medium in Cairo. She had married a French mechanic, and the couple wound up broke and stranded in the Orient at about the time that H.P.B. was making a success out of her Indian venture. Madame Coulomb wrote to H.P.B. asking for help, and astonishingly H.P.B. responded by inviting the Coulombs to India and giving them wide powers in the Theosophical Society.

H.P.B. never liked women very much, and Madame Coulomb was a particularly unlikable woman. Olcott and others constantly urged H.P.B. to get rid of her. But at least Madame Coulomb was one person with whom H.P.B. did not have to pretend. She could also be used on various errands, like delivering Mahatma letters. Her husband was clever with his hands and very useful for building the devices H.P.B. needed to produce her phenomena. That is why he was entrusted with the delicate and supersecret task of building the Shrine itself. The Shrine was a lacquered wooden cabinet, decorated with pictures of the Mahatmas, and hung from the ceiling of a tiny secret room, just off H.P.B.'s own bedroom. It functioned magnificently at first.

Just before the Shrine went into operation Olcott was a restless and unhappy man. But H.P.B. led him to the secret room and he was given the full treatment. The chelas prostrated themselves, there was a smell of incense and the doors to the Shrine were flung open revealing two slender vases, and a nice note of thanks from the Mahatmas to their loyal servant Henry S. Olcott. Olcott broke down and cried. After years of watching H.P.B.'s tricks he was still susceptible to them.

In 1884 H.P.B. was at the pinnacle of her international fame and glory. Branches of the Theosophical Society were flourishing in many parts of Europe and America. Madame decided it was time to return to Europe, but now she came in triumph. She was entertained at the best homes in France, England, and Germany, and though there were doubters they were not as numerous or as vocal as before. But back in India trouble was brewing. Without H.P.B.'s overpowering presence there was nothing to hold the strange and dissimilar group in the Adyar compound together. Most troublesome of all were the Coulombs. During her association with H.P.B. Madame Coulomb had collected some forty of her letters, and they were extremely damaging, for they gave instructions on how Madame Coulomb and her husband should arrange some of H.P.B.'s phenomena, like the "in the flesh" appearance of one of the Mahatmas.

After H.P.B.'s departure the Coulombs began muttering that the letters were for sale. Some of the theosophists advised H.P.B. to purchase them, while others attempted to lure the Coulombs out of the country. None of this worked and the Coulombs turned the letters over to the Christian missionaries, who had old scores to settle and who published them with glee.

H.P.B. naturally first denied writing the letters and hysterically claimed that the whole thing was a missionary plot to ruin her. But her style was unmistakable, and finally she admitted that she had written the letters but that Madame Coulomb had altered them in order to disort their meaning. Since everything H.P.B. wrote was rather convoluted, this line of defense satisfied some, but the publication of the Coulomb letters was still a damaging blow, and worse was to come.

While in London, H.P.B. was told that the Society for Psychical Research was going to send an investigator to Adyar to study the phenomena reported there. The members of the S.P.R. were generally sympathetic to all reports of alleged paranormal phenomena. Olcott and other true believers had enthusiastically agreed to the investigation, so H.P.B. could not refuse to cooperate. She even had to appear to welcome the investigation. But, in fact, she was badly frightened and toyed with the idea of running away, perhaps saying that she had been summoned to Tibet. But she hadn't the money on hand to disappear for a few years. So she slowly returned to

India where the S.P.R. investigator Richard Hodgson was already at work.

The Society for Psychical Research has a mixed record in investigating paranormal phenomena. Though some of its investigators have been credulous, almost all have been honest, and some have been brilliant. Hodgson was one of the brilliant ones. Later in his career he came to America, where he worked for the American Society for Psychical Research until his death in 1905. Many fraudulent mediums wished that he had never been born. When Hodgson went to Adyar he was a young man, fresh from Cambridge. He was a careful and patient investigator, and more than that he must have been a remarkable diplomat. Though his presence was not welcomed by everyone, he managed to get cooperation from most of those at Adyar. Even H.P.B. praised him as "an excellent, truthful, expert young man"—at least before his report was published. Since that time theosophists have expended millions of words attempting to prove that Hodgson was a liar, a knave, and a fool, but the charge just will not stick.

From the first, the Shrine made many sincere theosophists uncomfortable, since they suspected it might be a trick box. Before H.P.B. arrived back at Adyar a group of important European theosophists asked permission to examine it. The Indian chelas would not let them get near it. Finally, after veiled threats, the Indians reluctantly allowed them into the Shrine room. In appearance the cabinet called the Shrine looked innocent. One of the group struck the back of it with his hand and said with relief, "You see, it is quite solid," and at that moment a hidden panel flew open. This caused a general panic. After a day and a night of indecision, the theosophists chopped the guilty thing into little pieces and burned it. When Hodgson finally got into the Shrine room the Shrine itself was gone and all the walls had been replastered.

H.P.B. and other theosophists stumbled all over one another in an attempt to explain the secret panels. Some denied there were any movable parts at all. H.P.B. herself said that the movable panels made the Shrine easy to dismantle. A third explanation was that M. Coulomb had deliberately built the panels into the Shrine to incriminate theosophy.

For months Hodgson prowled about Adyar and the surrounding region. Anyone connected with theosophy was gently but thoroughly interrogated. Hodgson's report was published in the *Proceedings of the Society for Psychical Research* at the end of 1885. The evidence he had collected was overwhelming and devastating. The source of the report was also damaging to theosophy since the S.P.R. was well known to be partial to the paranormal. The Society did not actually endorse the report, for the group holds no corporate views, but they did publish it, and to many seriously interested in psychical research this seemed like an endorsement.

Hodgson had not been oblivious to the real power of Madame Blavatsky. He ended his report with this celebrated judgment:

"For our part, we regard her neither as the mouthpiece of hidden seers, nor as a mere vulgar adventuress; we think that she has achieved a title to permanent remembrance as one of the most accomplished, ingenious, and interesting impostors of history."

One of the most significant, yet generally overlooked aspects of the report is that while Hodgson found that H.P.B. had some conscious accomplices like the Coulombs, some of the Indian chelas and servants and some European mediums, most of those associated with her, including Olcott, were innocent of deliberate fraud. Hodgson did note, however, that the Colonel showed "extraordinary credulity and inaccuracy in observation and inference."

When H.P.B. returned to India from Europe, she was greeted by thousands of cheering students from the missionary schools. She was a European woman who had defended the Indians and who was now being attacked by other Europeans. Besides, the students didn't much care for their missionary teachers, and this was a fine way to put the needle to them.

At Adyar, however, her reception was not so warm. Many honest theosophists were deeply shocked by the Coulomb letters, though they might deny it in public. They were cooperating fully with Hodgson. Even the men who burned the Shrine confessed what they had done to the S.P.R. investigator. They were becoming increasingly aware that H.P.B. was a dishonest and perhaps dangerous woman. She was threatening to sue the missionaries, but her associates knew if she was ever put on the witness stand she would probably start denouncing the judge, and wind up in jail. Still, they could not bring themselves to abandon the movement. Instead, they decided that H.P.B. had to be quietly shunted aside and Olcott made head of the society. Worn out by the attacks upon her, and unable to think of an alternate plan, H.P.B. wearily agreed. She was hustled out of the country under an assumed name and apparently in a state of total collapse.

Shortly afterward, Damodar, her most trusted chela, disappeared. Some said he had gone to Tibet to join the Masters. There were rumors that he had undertaken the journey naked and had frozen to death in the mountains. Simple suicide is a more probable explanation for his disappearance.

H.P.B., accompanied by two servants, was installed in a small apartment in Italy. Safe from the storms at Adyar, but also without power, she began to recover and to scheme. Her mind probed wildly in all directions, and she sent off a flood of letters to all those whom she believed might help her. The man upon whom H.P.B. pinned her greatest hopes was Vsevolod S. Solovyoff, a Russian journalist. He seemed pliable enough at first, but he turned out to be anything but. When Solovyoff returned to Russia he had an affair with H.P.B.'s youngest sister, and found out a good deal about Madame's past. This was the unkindest possible cut and H.P.B. retaliated by spreading stories about Solovyoff's family. He warned her that he knew a thing or two, particularly about "old Blavatsky, whom you have prematurely buried."

This provoked one of H.P.B.'s greatest and most glorious explosions. In a long, hysterical, almost insane, yet strangely canny letter she threatened to write her own confession, in which she would ruin herself and practically everyone else she had ever come into contact with, including Solovyoff.

"I shall not spare myself, I swear I will not spare; *I myself will set fire* to the four quarters of my native wood; the society to wit, and I will perish, but I will perish *with a huge following.*"

Though this letter is often called H.P.B.'s "confession," she never really confessed to anything, she simply threatened to confess. "Even if all the filth, all the scandal and lies against me had been the holy truth, still I should have been no worse than hundreds of princesses, countesses, court ladies and royalties, than Queen Isabella herself, who have given themselves, even sold themselves to the entire male sex. . . .

". . . I will even take to lies, to the greatest of lies, which for that reason is the most likely of all to be believed. I will say and publish it in the *Times* and in all the papers, that the 'Master' and 'Mahatma K.H.' are only the product of my own imagination; that I invented them, that all the phenomena were all more or less spiritualistic apparitions and I shall have twenty million spiritists in a body at my back.

"I will say that in certain instances I fooled people; I will expose dozens of *fools, des hallucines . . .*"

H.P.B. wound up this letter with the postscript: "You may print this letter if you will, even in Russia. It is all the same now." Solovyoff did print the letter, but not until after Madame's death, when he published *A Modern Priestess of Isis,* a biography of H.P.B.

Though Madame had told Solovyoff that she would welcome death, it was an old line, one that she had used many times before. She was far from ready to give up. She commissioned Sinett to write her biography. Sinett was one of those grimly honest men for whom theosophy filled a deep and essential need. He had first met H.P.B. in India, where he was editor of the most powerful newspaper in the country. His unqualified support of theosophy cost him his job, and, finally disillusioned with H.P.B.'s antics, he returned to England. However, when H.P.B. called upon him for this new project he was again ready to serve her, and went through several difficult years, as Madame continually changed her mind about what she wanted included in her biography, and what she wanted left out. The result was not at all the lurid confession she had been threatening, but a sort of fairy tale in which she sought to cover up the activities of her twenty-five years as a wanderer with mysterious trips to Tibet and other meetings with the Mahatmas. Though the Mahatmas did not really appear until 1880, H.P.B. went to great lengths to establish their prior existence. After H.P.B.'s death poor

Sinett became totally disillusioned with her, but he continued to converse with the Mahatmas through mediums, and was ultimately reconciled with theosophy.

Although isolated from Adyar and all organized theosophy, thoroughly exposed by the Coulomb letters and the Hodgson report, and a genuinely ill woman without wealth (she was living on a small pension provided by Olcott), Madame still had the power to make important new converts and the energy to plan an ambitious project. Her most important disciple of this period was the Countess Constance Wachtmeister, an honest, intelligent, and hard-working woman who had been a spiritualist but was captivated by H.P.B. Countess Wachtmeister devoted several years to H.P.B.'s service, and was most responsible for getting her through this difficult period. H.P.B.'s new project was a book which ultimately came to be called *The Secret Doctrine*.

If Madame was a complete and conscious charlatan, as many believe, she was an extraordinarily hard-working one. For months she wrote from six in the morning until six in the evening with only short breaks for meals. She never wanted to go anywhere, and the Countess, who was shocked by H.P.B.'s total lack of physical activity, was only able to get her out of the house three times in six months.

The result of all this hard work was a pile of thousands of pages of manuscript. As it stood the manuscript was a hopeless and disorderly mess. H.P.B. could not possibly dream of having it published until it was thoroughly edited—and, more probably, entirely rewritten. Since this was exactly what had happened with *Isis Unveiled*, H.P.B. had anticipated this problem and had assumed that the most learned of her Indian followers, Subba Row, would "edit" the manuscript for her. But Subba Row had been badly shaken by the revelations of the Hodgson report. He resigned from the Theosophical Society and firmly refused to have anything to do with *The Secret Doctrine*. It was a hard blow, and might well have finished Madame's remarkable career if she had not received a stroke of good fortune. The Keightleys, two wealthy young Englishmen interested in occultism, turned up to see Madame. They not only offered to take her off to England and house her in their mansion, they also agreed to put the manuscript of *The Secret Doctrine* in shape for publication. This proved to be a hideously difficult task, and even when the book was published it remained pretty much of an incoherent jumble.

The popular press greeted *The Secret Doctrine* with the same sort of tolerant amusement that it displayed toward *Isis Unveiled*. Serious Oriental scholars were outraged by this vast and pretentious work. A California scholar, William Emmet Coleman spent years tracing H.P.B.'s gross errors and plagiarisms, for very little of the book was original. He and others concluded that H.P.B. had only the most superficial acquaintance with Oriental philosophy, and that most of the "information" in the book came from the works of other occultists or pseudo scientists of the day. According to H.P.B. *The Secret Doctrine* was based upon the now lost *Book of Dzyan* which was composed on the now lost continent of Atlantis. But most of what H.P.B. had to say about Atlantis was drawn directly, and without credit, from Ignatius Donnelly's crankish book *Atlantis: The Antediluvian World*.

The criticisms of Coleman and others who picked away at the facts and references in *The Secret Doctrine* were entirely beside the point. Real occultists do not read, or do not believe such critics. They loved the book, and they still do.

Before the Hodgson report, theosophy had commanded

the interest of some scientific-minded occultists—that is, individuals who believe that occult phenomena can and should be subjected to scientific testing. Hodgson himself admitted a strong prejudice in favor of theosophy before he started to investigate it. His report, however, was so devastating that all interest from this quarter simply stopped. But there have never been more than a small number of such individuals, while the vast majority of occultists are simple miracle seekers. Therefore, the resignations of the more intelligent theosophists did not really shake the movement. The mass waves of resignations and disillusionment that regularly swept the Theosophical Society were due more to personality conflicts between leading members, than to any recognition of fraud or foolishness.

In London, H.P.B. began to weave her old magic spells once again. She set up a branch of the Theosophical Society which was actually operating in competition with the London Lodge controlled by Olcott in Adyar. At the core of the Blavatsky Lodge was the Esoteric Section or E.S., a small handpicked group that had to pledge to obey all of Madame's orders without question or delay, and to maintain absolute secrecy. It was the sort of subservient and supersecret organization that has an unfortunately wide appeal even today. However, such organizations easily get out of hand. Within a year many of the members of the E.S. were thrown out, and a new and even more supersecret section, the Inner Group or I.G., was set up to guard the purity of theosophy.

Olcott was horrified at these goings on. He made two long trips from Adyar to London in an attempt to convince H.P.B. that she was doing great harm by splitting the movement. But since H.P.B. no longer depended on Olcott for money, she could afford to be arrogant, and she was. As usual, it was

Olcott who finally gave in. He returned to India, where he remained for the rest of his life, the more or less figurehead leader of the Theosophical Society.

It is difficult to know how deeply the fate or even survival of the Theosophical Society after her death actually concerned H.P.B. In 1889 she must have known that she had only a few years left to live. Most of the available theosophical leaders were old and weak like Olcott or worse. A promising figure was Dr. Elliott Coues of Washington, D.C., who had suddenly risen to power in the American branch of the Society (replacing General Abner Doubleday, the founder of baseball, who was also a longtime supporter of H.P.B.). But Dr. Coues refused to knuckle under to H.P.B. and he was soon attacking her in language as violent as her own. She was "fat, gross, of abominable habit and intolerable tempers, swearing like a pirate and smoking like a chimney." One of his attacks, printed in the New York *Sun,* was so intemperate that he even accused Madame of doing some things that she had not done (an admittedly difficult task). Madame demanded an apology, and finally after she was dead the *Sun* printed one. It was the closest thing to a public vindication that H.P.B. ever received.

The survival of the Theosophical Society was assured, however, when H.P.B. enlisted her last and greatest disciple, Annie Besant. Mrs. Besant was a woman almost as unconventional as H.P.B. herself. She had abandoned her vicar husband and vigorously taken up a variety of left-wing causes, including atheism. She was a brilliant, energetic and successful woman, who at the age of forty-two was a well-known public figure with a large personal following. But there was something missing from her life, and despite her avowal of atheism, she had begun to dabble in spiritualism and allied subjects. In 1889 Mrs. Besant was asked to review the two-volume *Secret Doctrine.* It was heavy going but the book fascinated her. In order to complete her article on the book, Mrs. Besant went to interview the author. H.P.B. charmed and captivated the younger woman in this first interview. As she was leaving, H.P.B. said to her, "Oh my dear Mrs. Besant, if you would only come among us!" Annie Besant was ready.

But before H.P.B. would accept Mrs. Besant she asked her to read Hodgson's damaging report on theosophy. H.P.B. knew her subject well. Later Mrs. Besant wrote: "Was the writer of the *Secret Doctrine* this miserable impostor, this accomplice of tricksters, this foul and loathsome deceiver, this conjurer with trap-doors and sliding panels." Sure she was, but Annie Besant would never believe that. "I laughed aloud at the absurdity and flung the Report aside with the righteous scorn of an honest nature that knew its own kind when it met them and shrank from the foulness and baseness of a lie."

H.P.B.'s total conquest of Annie Besant was perhaps her greatest achievement.

Rapidly, almost impulsively, H.P.B. began to turn over power in the Theosophical Society to Mrs. Besant. In the past H.P.B. had designated a dozen different individuals as her successor, and this was one of the reasons for the mad scramble for power that took place upon her death. Mrs. Besant, however, had many advantages—she was more energetic and intelligent than the other theosophical leaders, and she had H.P.B. in the flesh. Mrs. Besant moved the old lady into her spacious and sequestered house. There the incurable wanderer spent the final year of her life. Though she was now a total invalid, barely able to roll her own cigarettes, H.P.B. kept up a flow of papers and articles until just a few days before her death. The long-threatened confession that would rock the occult world never came. Instead, her words became more and more abstruse as she attempted not so much to justify her own life, but the existence of her creations, the Mahatmas. H.P.B. died quietly on May 8, 1891. The anniversary of her death is called White Lotus Day and is still observed by thousands of theosophists throughout the world.

One of H.P.B.'s former associates, Mabel Collins, paid her this tribute:

> I learned from her how foolish, how gullible, how easily flattered human beings are, taken *en masse.* Her contempt for her kind was on the same gigantic scale as everything else about her except her marvelously delicate tapering fingers. She had a greater power over the weak and credulous, a greater capacity for making black appear white, a larger waist, a more voracious appetite, a more ceaseless and insatiable hatred of those whom she judged to be her enemies, a greater disrespect for *les convenances,* a worse temper, a greater command of bad language, and a greater contempt for her fellow-men than I ever supposed possible to be contained in one person.

All in all, H.P.B. was a good deal larger than life size.

What was Helen Petrovna Blavatsky? Annie Besant once stated the problem very succinctly: "Either she is a messenger from the Masters or else she is a fraud." Mrs. Besant believed one explanation, but the evidence overwhelmingly points to the other. Is fraud the full explanation? It does not seem so. Both Richard Hodgson and Vsevolod Solovyoff indicated that H.P.B. might actually have been a Russian spy, and that this is why she had gone to India. But it hardly seems likely that even the Tsars' government would have been foolish enough to employ such an unreliable and hysterical secret agent.

I suspect that, though she was a cynical and thoroughly dishonest woman, H.P.B. was a genuine occultist, who really did believe that there were magical secrets to be had somewhere. At times she may well have believed in her own occult powers. The combination of cynic and true believer is not an uncommon one in occultism, and elsewhere for that matter. Frank Podmore, who met H.P.B. in London, said she seemed to have the ability to hypnotize her subjects. Perhaps she also had the ability to hypnotize herself.

CHAPTER IX

L. Ron Hubbard

"THE CREATION OF Dianetics is a milestone for Man comparable to his discovery of fire and superior to his inventions of the wheel and arch." So wrote Lafayette Ronald Hubbard, the man who created Dianetics. "Dianetics," he continued, "is an exact science and its application is on the order of, but simpler than, engineering. Its axioms should not be confused with theories since they demonstrably exist as natural laws hitherto undiscovered."

Hubbard's first creation—dianetics—thus was a science, or, as its numerous detractors claimed, a pseudo science. Though the introduction of dianetics in 1950 did not quite revolutionize the world as did the discovery of fire, it made a surprisingly large splash, considering that it had come from almost nowhere.

Hubbard's book *Dianetics: The Modern Science of Mental Health* sold thousands of copies. Although it was panned by virtually all serious reviewers who bothered with it at all and was roundly denounced by physicians and scientists alike, it did attract a few notable converts, at first. But we must point out that practically every strange belief does.

I can recall that several of my neighbors had formed a dianetic study group, and they were busily practicing dianetic therapy on one another. The technique was simple enough. In fact Hubbard extolled the utter simplicity of dianetics, claiming that after reading his book any two reasonably intelligent people could master the technique and practice it successfully.

What could dianetics do for you? Hubbard said that through dianetic therapy some seventy percent of all human ailments could be cured—because seventy percent of all human ailments were psychosomatic. At first my neighbors said that dianetics was really "helping" and that they "felt better." Eventually over a couple of months they got new ailments, or the old ones reasserted themselves, or they just got bored with the whole thing and drifted away from dianetics. Today, if they are reminded of their former flirtation with dianetics, they find it a bit embarrassing and pass the incident off as a youthful folly. The same sort of disappointment overtook dianetics converts all over the country. It seemed to me, from my limited perspective, that dianetics, which so obviously was unable to live up to its grandiose claims, would soon fade away entirely.

Years later in New York City I was riding with a particularly talkative cabbie who was explaining to me the virtues of a new religion called scientology. I had never heard of scientology before, but some of the terminology sounded familiar, and as he rattled on I slowly realized that dianetics had not disappeared after all. It had merely been transformed, enlarged, and renamed scientology. L. Ron Hubbard's brain child was and is very much of a going concern, and while scientology does not have the broad appeal that dianetics once had, its converts are more committed and more fanatical.

The transformation of the "exact science" of dianetics to the "religion" of scientology took some rather agile mental and semantic gymnastics on Hubbard's part. Even today some scientologists are not entirely comfortable with the "religion" label that they have placed upon themselves. Besides, if you claim to be a scientist who can cure all sorts of diseases, and that is certainly what the practitioners of dianetics first claimed, then you are liable to get into all manner of legal troubles, and that is just what happened.

As a religion scientology is protected under the religious freedom sections of the Constitution, and while scientologists still regularly run afoul of the law there is little doubt that the religion claim has given them a measure of protection.

Hubbard has stated that one of the reasons that scientology became a religion "is that a society accords to men of the church an access not given to others. Prisons, hospitals, and institutions . . . cannot do otherwise than welcome men of the church . . ."

But scientology really *is* a religion, faith, or, if those names seem too grand, a cult. And the inventor, chief guru, and absolute dictator of the tight little world of scientology is L. Ron Hubbard. He didn't rediscover fire, but Hubbard can claim the honor of having added a new dimension to the modern occult scene.

Who is L. Ron Hubbard? The question is not so easy to answer. He was born in 1911 in Tilden, Nebraska. But even that rather ordinary statement has proved impossible to check, and everything else about Hubbard's life is even less certain. His father may have been Commander H. R. Hubbard, U.S.N. Hubbard has also publicized his hereditary connection with an old aristocratic English family, but this may be entirely mythical.

One of Hubbard's semiofficial biographies (which he may have written himself) says that he lived on his grandfather's Montana ranch until he was ten. According to the biography, "he could ride before he could walk." Later, at the age of about twelve, he traveled with his family to Washington, D.C.

He was probably in the navy, or it may have been the marines. Hubbard briefly attended George Washington University Engineering School in Washington, D.C. He was not graduated because he flunked freshman physics and failed to return to the University. He never seems to have held a real engineering job. Much later Hubbard apparently picked up a degree from something called Sequoia University.

Before his unhappy experience with George Washington University, Hubbard's biography claims that he traveled widely, particularly in Asia. He became familiar with those secrets of the East so dear to the hearts of all occultists. However, during those years when he was supposed to have been traveling in the Orient, one investigator of Hubbard's tangled past discovered that he was actually attending Helena High School in Helena, Montana, and, after that, Woodward School for Boys, a YMCA preparatory school in Washington, D.C.

After his nongraduation from George Washington University, Hubbard's biography states that he led several expeditions into Central America, "all of them undertaken to study savage peoples and cultures." In fact, Hubbard is a duly elected member of the Explorers Club in New York. The club is pretty choosy about its members, and presumably checked Hubbard's credentials as a bona fide explorer, though they will not open their records to public inspection.

During this same period Hubbard also picked up a pilot's license and seems to have made himself a bit of a reputation as a daredevil flier. He also apparently sang and played banjo on a radio program.

It is no longer possible to separate truth from fiction in this part of Hubbard's life. The waters have been too muddied and the problem is an academic one in any case. The overwhelming and uncontestable fact about Ron Hubbard's career was that in the late thirties he began writing, and for years he was an enormously prolific writer of pulp fiction and articles. He also wrote some movie and radio scripts.

Hubbard's first novel, *Buckskin Brigade,* appeared in 1937, but he did not reach top form until he discovered the science fiction pulps. His first stories began to appear in *Astounding Science Fiction* in 1938. And for the next fifteen years Hubbard's stories under half a dozen different pseudonyms popped up in most of the regular science fiction magazines. Some of Hubbard's stories like "Slaves of Sleep," "Typewriter in the Sky," and "Fear" were really quite good, and they moved Hubbard into the front rank of science fiction writers of the late 1940s.

Hubbard's writing speed was legendary, even among pulp writers who were paid by the word and thus turned out words at an unbelievable rate. He was said to compose his stories on a continuous roll of paper, using a specially constructed electric typewriter with single keys for such common words as "and" and "the" in order to save typing time. The estimates of the number of published words that Hubbard actually turned out varies widely, but it was in the millions—not a record by any means, but it is impressive. It is commonly reported that he wrote the thick manuscript for his book on dianetics in three weeks, and it certainly reads as if he did. There is little doubt that L. Ron Hubbard was a great typist.

The science fiction fans of the late '40s and early '50s were a fanatical lot. I know, because I was one of them. The bond between the S.F. fan and the writer and editor of science fiction was a deep and personal one—at least the fan thought it was. Writers and editors, I suspect, took a more business-like view of the whole thing. We fans were passionately attached to the magazines we read, and we tended to regard them as something beyond entertainment, and beyond fiction. We believed that science fiction writers were true prophets of the future.

Some science fiction writers and editors were afflicted with a similar delusion. At least a couple writers had, and still have, grotesquely inflated conceptions of themselves as prophets and teachers. Ray Palmer, the editor of *Amazing Science Fiction* at this time, began to promote something called "the Great Shaver Mystery," the wild and weird ramblings of a Pennsylvania welder named Richard S. Shaver. It was all about lost continents and underground civilizations. In 1947 Palmer went on to promote flying saucers through his magazine and, in fact, Ray Palmer, more than any other single individual, was responsible for the flying saucer mania that gripped this country for two decades and threatens to erupt once again, at almost any moment.

While Palmer promoted ideas that often smacked of mysticism, the late John Campbell, editor of *Astounding Science Fiction* (now *Analog*) liked to promote way-out technology, or what he considered technology. Campbell was unquestionably a fine editor, as well as a pretty good writer. He edited his magazine for nearly thirty years, and was one of the prime moving forces of the development of science fiction in America. Campbell was also a great American character, and a prickly supporter of odd causes and theories.

In 1950 Hubbard approached Campbell with his dianetics idea. Dianetics was based more or less on the conception that the human mind was a perfect computer, and the only thing that it needed was reprogramming in order to return to a perfect state. This appealed mightily to Campbell's technological instinct. In May 1950, Campbell wrote an enthusiastic editorial about dianetics. This was the first public mention of the subject. When Hubbard's book on dianetics appeared a few months later the science fiction fans were eager to get at it, and the book went through several printings in just a few months. Campbell contributed an appendix on "the Scientific Method" to Hubbard's book.

Soon, however, dianetics lost its appeal among the hard core of science fiction fans. Many became openly hostile to it. At a science fiction fans' convention in the early fifties, the name of L. Ron Hubbard was roundly cursed. Campbell himself drifted away, or perhaps the break was more explosive.

At first the popularity of dianetics grew so rapidly that psychiatrists and psychologists were caught a little off balance. In September of 1950 the American Psychological Association called upon psychologists not to use dianetic therapy, and said that they were "suspending judgment" on the treatment, until further information could be obtained. The statement pointed out that Hubbard's book contained absolutely no documentation of its claims.

Hubbard moved rapidly. Within a few months he had established several dianetic research foundations that offered courses in dianetics. Why one had to take courses in dianetics, when Hubbard had stated flatly in his book that the subject could easily be learned by studying the book, was never made clear. In any case, the dianetics courses cost several hundred dollars.

But the authorities were beginning to take an increasingly suspicious view of L. Ron Hubbard and dianetics. Hubbard's New Jersey foundation shut down quickly. The Dianetic Research Foundation in Wichita went bankrupt.

Out in California, where he was lecturing to huge audiences, Hubbard staged what can only be termed a classic public disaster. He introduced a young lady named Sonya Bianca as a "clear." This was the highest state of mental development according to dianetic theory. Sonya Bianca was not only supposed to be totally without neurosis and psychosomatic ailments, she was also supposed to possess total recall and have the ability to knock off someone's hat at fifty feet, by just thinking about it. Before six thousand people at the Los Angeles Shrine Auditorium, Sonya Bianca was unable even to remember the color of Hubbard's tie when his back was turned. The audience proved remarkably gentle. They didn't throw anything—they just left.

At about this time Hubbard's second wife divorced him, claiming he was a "paranoid schizophrenic" and that he subjected her to "systematic torture." This was the extreme language of the divorce courts, but the case was well publicized and did not help Hubbard's cause.

Some followers defected and set up on their own. In Wichita a group of businessmen purchased Hubbard's bankrupt foundation and started pushing their own brand of dianetics. Early in the 1950s the science writer Martin Gardner observed, "At the time of writing, the dianetics craze seems to have burned itself out as quickly as it caught fire. . . ."

He continued, "At the moment, the founder of dianetics is living in Phoenix, Arizona. From there the Hubbard Association of Scientologists ('scientology' is a new Hubbardian term, meaning the 'science of knowledge') is mailing out literature fulminating against the Wichita group . . ."

Anyone who believed that Hubbard would be crushed by the many blows which befell him in 1951 and 1952 did not count on the man's resiliency and energy. But before we discuss the transformation of L. Ron Hubbard from "discoverer" of the "new science" of dianetics to high priest and perhaps messiah of the new "religion" of scientology, we had better say a few words about what dianetics purported to be.

The basic concepts of dianetics are, as Hubbard claimed, quite simple, and even simple-minded. They are made more difficult to understand and thus presumably more impressive by a complex terminology invented by Hubbard. This sort of jargon is quite familiar to occultists, politicians, military men, professors, and all too many others.

As already pointed out, a basic dianetic concept was that the mind is a perfect computer. But part of the mind receives impressions that are recorded literally. This part of the mind, called the "reactive mind" by Hubbard, does not "think about" anything. It receives these impressions called engrams, even when sleeping, unconscious, or before a person is born. Many of these engrams are very literal, and they can create all manner of problems in later life.

Here is an example: A pregnant woman is constipated. As she strains for a bowel movement, this painfully compresses the embryo in her womb. This creates an engram. The embryo also records, as an engram, his mother saying, "Oh this is hell. I am all jammed up inside. I feel stuffy. I can't think. This is too terrible to be borne." Later in life, these engrams cause the patient to have constant colds, "I feel stuffy . . ." and a severe inferiority complex, "too terrible to be *born*."

If you think that pun is bad, Hubbard uses a worse one in telling about a patient who had a chronic rash on her backside. This had been caused by her mother's frequent requests for aspirin. This had been impressed upon the patient's literal reactive mind as "ass burn."

Hubbard's view of human behavior is rather horrifying. Reading *Dianetics, The Modern Science of Mental Health* one gets the impression that husbands routinely and severely beat their pregnant wives, and that the average pregnant woman attempts twenty or thirty abortions with knitting needles. Needless to say, the beatings and attempted abortions produce some pretty harmful engrams on the unborn child who is experiencing the whole thing. That is why we are all so neurotic.

In order to get rid of these harmful engrams, the patient had to go through a period of dianetic therapy known as auditing. The patient sits or lies down while the therapist, called the auditor, prompts him to go back along his "time track." As he returns to the early engram-forming experiences he is able to talk about them, and thus they lose their power to create problems. When all the engrams are erased a person is called a "clear." The "clear" is not only free of all psychosomatic ailments and neuroses, he is also smarter and stronger than the ordinary person.

Hubbard's concept of a world in which dianetics would be routinely practiced has some rather disturbing overtones. Writing in *Astounding Science Fiction,* Hubbard revealed that since the "clears" would be superior people, ". . . one sees with some sadness that more than three quarters of the world's population will become subject to the remaining quarter as a natural consequence and about which we can do exactly nothing." Of course, since the clears will be by nature good, they will order the world for the best. The same claim has been advanced by "master race" theorists from time immemorial.

Where did Hubbard get all his inspirations for dianetics? In his book, and others he wrote on the subject, he talks a great deal of "extensive research," but not the slightest evidence of any research at all is given. Nothing Hubbard has ever written bears any resemblance to a scientific document, not because of the ideas expressed, but because of the way in which the information is presented. Hubbard simply makes flat statements about what is. These are sometimes illustrated by little stories, like the one about the aspirin. There is, in short, simply no way of checking out Hubbard's facts. You either take them or leave them.

To compound the mystery of the origin of dianetics, Hubbard introduced a work called *Excalibur*. According to Hubbard, *Excalibur* was a book that contained all the "basic principles of human existence." An advertisement for the book published in the early 1950s states that Hubbard first wrote *Excalibur* in 1938. But, "When four of the first fifteen people who read it went insane, Mr. Hubbard withdrew it and placed it in a vault where it has remained until now. Copies to selected readers only and then on signature. Released only on sworn statement not to permit other readers to read it. Contains data not to be released during Mr. Hubbard's stay on earth. The complete fast formula for clearing. The secret not even Dianetics disclosed. Facsimile of original, individually typed for manuscript buyer. Gold-bound and locked. Signed by author. Very limited. Per copy . . . $1,500.00."

There were no known buyers, indeed there is some confusion as to whether any manuscript called *Excalibur* has ever existed. The book that men could not read without going insane was a private joke among writers of science fiction and fantasy, long before Hubbard latched onto it. There are conflicting stories as to when and how *Excalibur* was written. Hubbard's advertising copy for the book says he wrote it in 1938, and it was the result of his expeditions among "the savage peoples of the world" and other researches. An article in one of the science fiction fan magazines tells a somewhat different, and more amazing story. According to this article Hubbard told his fans he received the inspiration for *Excalibur* while he was dead. Says the article, Hubbard "died" for eight minutes in 1948 during an operation performed on him for injuries he had received while in the navy.

"Hubbard realized that while he was dead, he had received a tremendous inspiration, a great Message which he must impart to others. He sat at his typewriter for six days and nights and nothing came out—then *Excalibur* emerged. *Excalibur* contains the basic metaphysical secrets of the universe. He sent it around to some publishers; they all hastily rejected it . . . He locked it away in a bank vault. But then, later, he informed us he would try publishing a 'diluted' version of it . . . Dianetics, I was recently told by a friend of Hubbard's, is based upon one chapter of *Excalibur.*"

Anyone familiar with the development of occultism will recognize the pattern immediately. Occultists love "secret" books which are too "hot" to be published. The "truth" they contain is revealed a bit at a time. If at any time the revealed "truth" seems less than satisfactory, the occult master can explain that it only seems so because he has been "prevented" from revealing the full truth. This particular gimmick works better than one could possibly believe.

After the collapse of the initial dianetics bubble, Hubbard was a whirlwind of activity, turning out books and creating organizations at a bewilderingly rapid rate. He started something called Hubbard College in which he taught all the courses and gave out degrees of "Registered Dianeticist." In Kansas he organized Scientific Press, Inc., which published and distributed his books. In Phoenix there was the Hubbard Association of Scientologists (HAS).

In 1953 Hubbard had moved the center of his activities to Philadelphia, and that year he also established the first branch of the HAS in London. Scientology failed to catch on in the East at first, and Hubbard returned once again to Phoenix, where he added a graduate school to the Hubbard College, and incorporated the Hubbard Association of Scientologists International (HASI).

Although Hubbard's theories expanded dramatically after he introduced dianetics, in the early 1950s he was still basically peddling dianetics. From the point of view of someone who wished to enroll in one of Hubbard's courses or otherwise practice his therapy, the biggest difference was the introduction of the Electropsychometer or E-Meter. This little device, which cost the student about one hundred dollars, was considered essential to all dianetic therapy, and has become a standard part of the "religion" of scientology.

Basically, the E-Meter can be thought of as a very simplified form of lie detector. The patient grasps two handles, and the machine passes a weak electric current through his body. The body's electrical resistance changes, and these changes are registered on the dial of the E-Meter, which is being watched by the auditor. If the needle is jumping around while a particular subject is being discussed, then the auditor assumes that the subject causes problems. He keeps on asking questions about it (or repeating the same question) until the needle stops jumping around. According to a brochure on the machine it registers "relative degrees of dynamic psychophysical stress from moment to moment during the Dianetic session."

Since the E-Meter was part of a process which was reputed to cure diseases, it was a rather risky device. The Food and Drug Administration tends to get pretty hard-nosed about such devices and they began taking a close and unfriendly look at the E-Meter. In 1963 the government finally got a court order approving the seizure of E-Meters and books relating to them.

Hubbard had seen this coming and tried to avoid the calamity by stating that the E-Meter was used only to "disclose truth to the individual who is being processed and thus free him spiritually," no matter what it had been used for previously. The E-Meter he contended "is a valid religious instrument, used in Confessionals, and is in no way diagnostic and does not treat." All E-Meters were labeled "The E-Meter is not intended or effective for the diagnosis, treatment, or prevention of any disease." This label reminds one of the warnings that appear on cigarette packs.

The E-Meter case kicked around in the courts for several years, but finally in 1969 the United States Court of Appeals decided that there was no way to prove that scientology was not a religion, and that the E-Meters were not valid articles of worship. So the blanket of religious freedom had worked very well in this instance.

While the FDA investigation and the court cases dragged on Hubbard had not been inactive. Some of the old dianetics groups that had broken away from Hubbard had faltered badly without his guiding spirit. By 1955 most of those that were still active were begging to get back under Hubbard's new umbrella, scientology. A "Unification Congress" was held. Hubbard now claimed that scientology was the original name of his theory, but that he had changed it to dianetics in order to make a test of its popularity. With the test a success, the original name could be restored.

The big break from the dianetics of the early fifties came in 1955. Then Hubbard and his new wife, Mary Sue, moved to Washington, D.C., and established The Founding Church of Scientology. Auditors began calling themselves ministers, and some adopted clerical garb. Under the protection of religious freedom, L. Ron Hubbard and his expanding flock prospered.

Through it all Hubbard was able to run a very tight ship. There were defectors, but none ever really threatened Hubbard's absolute control over his brain child. In order to survive the attacks, the ridicule, the bankruptcies, the government investigations, and the endless shifting from place to place, L. Ron Hubbard had to be pretty tough. Often his toughness showed through in rather ominous ways.

For years Hubbard has been conducting a war against psychologists and psychiatrists. This is hardly surprising, since he has been almost unanimously denounced from that quarter.

The late Dr. William Menninger of the Menninger Clinic of Topeka, Kansas, said that Hubbard's system and ideas "can potentially do a great deal of harm."

Hubbard has written, "The psychiatrist and his front groups operate straight out of the terrorist text books. The Mafia looks like a convention of Sunday School teachers compared to these terrorist groups."

In order to "spread the good word" about scientology, Hubbard encouraged his "ministers" to adopt methods that were downright crude. For example, he advised them to read newspapers in order to get the names and addresses of persons who had been injured, or families in which there had been a death or serious illness. They were then to hotfoot it over to the person's home. "He [the representative of scientology] should represent himself to the person or the person's family as a minister whose compassion was compelled by the newspaper story concerning the person. He should then enter the presence of the person and give a nominal assist, leaving his card which states exactly where church services are held every Sunday and with the statement that much fuller recovery is possible by coming to these free services takes his departure." When you realize that very little about scientology is free, and that anyone who gets hooked on it is pushed to spend hundreds of dollars, then this "Casualty Contact," as Hubbard blandly labeled the technique, seems a pretty grim and ruthless practice.

Today the Casualty Contact has been abandoned, but the Church of Scientology remains a high-pressure, hard-sell outfit. The most casual inquiry will bring a flood of printed material, along with friendly little personal notes and occasionally phone calls. If you want your mailbox full for months, just contact your nearest scientology headquarters. In New York City, at least, scientology advertises itself with garish Day-Glo posters in the subway encouraging the passerby to "Join the world of the Totally Free." Occasionally girls pass out free tickets for scientology lectures and services on street corners. In person scientology representatives are more persistent than the hungriest insurance agent you have ever met. All of this was part of a policy that Hubbard established very early.

It is also not wise to fall too far behind in your payments to scientology. If you do, you will first get a few nasty letters, and then your notes will be turned over to a regular collection agency.

Just how much money scientology has made for L. Ron Hubbard is a matter of some dispute. The whole operation was under his complete control and his wife handled the accounts. There were no nosy stockholders to demand a public audit. Disgruntled former scientologists claim that Hubbard has been made a multimillionaire. There is talk of money in secret Swiss bank accounts and so forth. Hubbard denies this and claims he has made nothing from scientology. He says that any money he may have has come from his years as a popular writer. There is little doubt, however, that heading scientology has been a lot more profitable than turning out pulp science fiction. But Hubbard's wealth has also undoubtedly been exaggerated by his opponents. Outsiders generally tend to exaggerate the amount of money that even a successful cult leader can accumulate.

In March of 1959 Hubbard decided to abandon Washington, D.C., and the United States entirely, and set up his international headquarters in England. This marked the beginning of yet another phase in his colorful career. But before we go on to that, we had better pause for a moment and find out what Hubbard had been pushing all of these years. What is scientology? What is its appeal?

It would be hopeless and useless to try to summarize all of L. Ron Hubbard's theories of scientology because they have changed constantly over the years. Besides they just don't make any sense. I might qualify that by saying to the rational outsider they don't make any sense, but like all mystical ideas they make perfect and divine sense to those who accept them. One experiences a curious sensation after reading scientological literature, or talking to a confirmed scientologist. The words used are mostly familiar, and rather simple, and thus unlike the long obscure words often employed by mystical groups. But it does not take long to realize that words do not mean the same thing to a scientologist and non-scientologist. The scientologist uses language to awe, to impress, and to confuse, not to explain. In order to really "understand" what is being said, one must make a "leap of faith."

But one can discern among the millions of words written about scientology, one very familiar concept—the immortality of the soul. It is the immensely comforting thought that you will never die that forms a basic part of the appeal of scientology. Naturally Hubbard invents his own words. Instead of the soul, he talks of the Theatan.

According to Hubbard, "Theatan is the word given to the awareness of awareness unit, the life source, the personality, and the beingness of *homo-sapiens* . . . It is the person . . . The Theatan is a glowing unit of energy source. He seems to himself to be anything from a quarter of an inch to two inches in diameter. His capability is knowing and being. He exudes and uses energy in many forms. He can perceive and handle energy flows easily. The Theatan enters some time in infancy. This may be before, during or following birth. He comes in a state of personal unknowingness, desiring to have an identity which he considers he has not without a body . . ."

Reincarnation also figures heavily in Hubbard's scientological universe. The Theatan has lived in other bodies in other times and on other planets and will do so again after the death of its current "meat body." Some of the problems that crop up in this life are really hangovers from things that happened to the Theatan during its many-trillion-year sojourn through time and space. If, however, the Theatan gets cleared by scientology during its time on earth, then it will face all its future lives free of aberrations. This seems vaguely akin to the concept of Nirvana.

Hubbard, however, cannot be accused of total unoriginality. He has festooned these core ideas with an astonishing array of highly imaginary material that seems to have come straight out of his old pulp science fiction writing days. One of his wildest additions is the Gorilla Goals. While the Theatans are between bodies they are sent to "implant stations" on various planets. Here they are implanted with a variety of goals. The Gorilla Goals were implanted in an amusement park setting many trillions of years ago. Writes Hubbard:

"The symbol of a Gorilla was always present in the place where the goal was given. Sometimes a large gorilla, black, was seen elsewhere in the park. A mechanical or live gorilla was always seen in the park. This activity was conducted by the Hoipolloi, a group of operators in meat body societies. They were typical carnival people. They let out concessions for these Implant 'Amusement Parks.' A pink-striped white shirt with sleeve garters was the uniform of the Hoipolloi. Such a figure often rode on the roller coaster cars. Monkeys were also used on the cars."

Now all of this business about Gorilla Goals and Hoipolloi is so silly that it seems an obvious put-on. Is Hubbard saying, if the suckers will swallow this they will swallow anything? Or is it an in joke for all scientologists? Perhaps they enjoy watching outsiders fuss and fume over such silliness.

Another idea that appears more or less consistently in the millions of words that Hubbard has written about scientology is that reality is a creation of the mind or the Theatan. He wrote:

"Considerations take rank over the mechanics of space, energy, and time. By this it is meant that an idea or opinion is fundamentally superior to space, energy, and time, or organizations of form, since it is conceived that space, energy, and time are themselves broadly agreed upon considerations. That so many minds agree brings about Reality in the form of space, energy, and time. These mechanics, then of space, energy and time, are the products of agreed-upon considerations mutually held by life." Of course, there is nothing original about this idea either. The issue was stated much more eloquently and briefly over two hundred years ago by Bishop George Berkeley.

"All the choir of heaven and furniture of earth—in a word, all those bodies which compose the mighty frame of the world —have not any subsistence without a mind."

This sort of subjective idealism is quite unarguable, but not particularly fashionable today. Whether this is a seriously held idea for Hubbard, or merely a convenient philosophical harbor in which to drop anchor during a stormy argument, is impossible to say. But if there is any consistency at all in L. Ron Hubbard's philosophy, it seems to be the supremacy of the mind.

When Hubbard moved his headquarters to England in 1959, scientology was already well established there. He purchased a baronial estate called Saint Hill Manor just outside of East Grinsted in Sussex. Saint Hill Manor had been built in 1728 and had once belonged to the Maharaja of Jaipur. At Saint Hill, Hubbard was inaccessible to all but invited guests.

I talked to a reporter for the *Saturday Evening Post* who went to Saint Hill to do a story about Hubbard and scientology. The reporter vividly remembered that each afternoon a butler in full livery brought the master his afternoon Coca-Cola on a silver tray.

Even in this splendid isolation Hubbard was able to keep firm control of scientology's world-wide organization. All important decisions were made by Hubbard personally. He maintained instant communication with the main scientology centers by means of an extensive Telex network. In addition, Hubbard's famed ability to grind out thousands of words a week never deserted him. He turned out an endless stream of bulletins, letters, policy reports, pamphlets, and books. He also recorded lectures on tape which were played at scientology meetings around the world, and could be purchased for home listening.

But the more scientology grew, the more obvious a target it became for its many enemies. Scientology had been brought to Australia in the mid-1950s and had prospered there. (Scientology has done well only in English-speaking countries, possibly because Hubbardian jargon is untranslatable.) When Hubbard visited Australia in 1959 he was received warmly. When he returned, he declared that Australia would probably be the first totally "clear" continent in the world. But in the state of Victoria, where scientology was particularly well established, the press began attacking it, and cries were raised for a government investigation. A Board of Inquiry was set up.

At first scientologists welcomed the Board of Inquiry. Hubbard even indicated that this board had been his idea. But very soon the scientologists began to realize that the investigation was not going the way they wished it to. In May of 1964, just prior to the Victoria state elections, scientologists declared war on the Australian Labour Party, claiming that the party was hostile to scientology.

The Victoria investigation was exhaustive, and its published conclusions were as negative as they could possibly be: In 1965 the state of Victoria passed an act that in essence banned the practice of scientology. The police moved in on the scientology headquarters in Melbourne and seized thousands of personal files.

Hubbard was beside himself with rage. "The foundation of Victoria," he fulminated in a booklet entitled "Kangaroo Court," "consists of the riff-raff of London's slums, robbers, murderers, prostitutes, fences, thieves . . . This insane attack on Scientology can best be understood if Victoria is seen for what it is—a very primitive community, somewhat barbaric with a rudimentary knowledge of the physical sciences. In fact, it is a scientific barbarism so bigoted that they know not and do not know they are ignorant."

For a while it appeared as though other Australian states might follow the lead of Victoria in banning scientology. But this did not happen. Even some of the outspoken opponents of scientology believed that the Victoria action was a much too harsh response to a minor problem. In New South Wales the opinion was expressed that a ban on scientology would be "like using a sledgehammer to crack a walnut." Still, the dream of Australia as the first totally clear continent had been shattered beyond repair.

Probably the most potentially disastrous development for scientology started in 1966, for it was then that the United States Internal Revenue Bureau began examining the tax-exempt status of scientology.

In the summer of 1969 scientology lost a major appeal

against the I.R.S. decision to revoke its tax exemption. To date the case is still in the courts, and there are numerous legal channels still open for scientology's lawyers. But the outlook is not brilliant. A decision against scientology's tax exemption might pretty well break the organization in the United States, at least financially. The Church of Scientology could be handed a bill for back taxes dating from 1956, with an added six percent interest.

Nor has scientology's status in England remained tranquil. The residents of East Grinsted were becoming openly alarmed about Saint Hill and the stream of scientologists from around the world who kept going up to the place. Another ominous sign to the people of East Grinsted was that Hubbard was buying other property in the area. Was scientology planning to "take over" the village? Embarrassing questions were raised in Parliament.

Finally in 1968 the British government did move against scientology. Foreign nationals were no longer allowed to come to England to study scientology on student visas, nor were work permits to be issued to any foreign national who was to work for the scientology organization. Some eight hundred scientologists were barred from entering England to attend a scientology conference in August 1968. These relatively moderate measures, however, did not satisfy the people of East Grinsted, who wanted to see Saint Hill closed down entirely. So far, no direct government moves have been made against Englishmen who practice or learn scientology.

The British government did study the group, and Kenneth Robertson, the Minister of Health, delivered a stinging indictment of scientology in the House of Commons. "Its authoritarian principles and practices are a potential menace to the personality and well-being of those so deluded as to become its followers," he said.

Either Hubbard had anticipated what was going to happen in England, or he was simply driven by his restless energy to move on to something and somewhere new. In 1966 he announced that he was retiring from scientology entirely. He sold his interests and left England ostensibly for retirement in Rhodesia. Soon he was back in England, and it was rumored that the Rhodesian government had hurried him on his way.

Trouble in Australia, trouble in the United States, trouble in England, even trouble in Rhodesia—where to go? Then Hubbard made his most dramatic move of all. If he was to be a prophet without honor in all countries, then he would live in no country. He had purchased a fleet of ships, most of them old and rather rundown, but still seaworthy. Collectively the fleet was called the *Sea Org* (Organization). Hubbard and his little scientological fleet have been sailing around mostly in Mediterranean waters for the past few years. But even here they have not been safe from hostility. The Spanish government made the coast of Spain an unwelcome harbor. In 1969 Hubbard's fleet made the Greek island of Corfu its home base until March, when the Greek government abruptly gave Hubbard and some two hundred followers on the ships twenty-four hours to get out of Corfu.

At the time of this writing Hubbard is still aboard ship somewhere, and clearly thinking of expanding this aspect of the scientology operation, for there are a couple of scientological ships anchored off the coast of California. These presumably will be the nucleus of the projected Pacific *Sea Org*.

From shipboard Hubbard still seems to personally control scientology's world-wide organization, despite his announced retirement. What the future holds for L. Ron Hubbard and his brainchild of scientology is quite impossible to predict. But we can say that despite attacks from all sides scientology is still very much of a going concern. Scientologists claim that they have at least a hundred thousand members throughout the world, and as many as a million on the fringes of the movement, and that it is growing rapidly. These figures may not be greatly exaggerated.

You might guess that scientology would appeal mainly to the little-old-lady-in-tennis-shoes type. Its basic attraction would still seem to be a cure for what ails you, and the older you get the more there is that ails you. But a visit to the scientology offices in New York City would dispel that stereotype. Most of those around the offices are young and hip-looking. They are searching not so much for a cure to a physical ailment, but for the "total freedom" promised in all the scientology ads.

It would be highly unwise to predict that scientology will simply disappear if its tax exemption does. It seems to be firmly grounded and filling some deep needs. Scientology will probably be around for quite a while.

One cannot leave the subject of L. Ron Hubbard and scientology without mentioning the most controversial aspect of this obviously controversial subject—that is "ethics," though perhaps discipline or punishment might be more accurate words.

Ex-scientologists, and there are plenty of them, some quite bitter, circulate the wildest rumors about what can happen to someone who openly opposes scientology. They are imprisoned aboard a *Sea Org* ship; there is a special prison in Brooklyn for defecting scientologists; some have been mysteriously murdered, and so forth. When one high-ranking scientologist left the organization in a dispute over the harshness of ethics, he was convinced that the Ethics Squad was trying to kidnap him, and he was forced to travel to his home in South Africa in disguise.

There is no evidence at all to support the rumors that Hubbard has ever used physical force of any kind against his opponents. But Hubbard's statements over the years about what should be done to those who oppose scientology create an atmosphere in which such rumors can be widely circulated and believed.

Said Hubbard: "They [those who oppose scientology] are declared enemies of mankind, the planet, and all life. They are fair game. No amnesty may ever cover them."

Scientologists once had to answer fairly elaborate security questionnaires, and took all manner of loyalty oaths. Hubbard also quite openly encourages members to spy on one another, and report what they find to higher authorities. It is helpful to recall that the formative years of dianetics coincided with the powerful years of Senator Joe McCarthy, when such techniques were popular. McCarthy's success seems to have left a lasting impression on Hubbard's mind.

Hubbard has, incidentally, also always maintained a strongly anti-communist position. He claimed that in 1938 the Russians tried to lure him over to their side with a huge bribe, but that he refused and as a result they robbed his apartment. He has also claimed that more recently Fidel Castro wanted to send a special team of men to Saint Hill for scientological training, but that he turned Castro down.

Most of what Hubbard says about punishing his enemies is empty talk. But he does have some real power over those within the organization—not the power to throw people into a mythical jail but to cut them off from their friends and associates by a policy called disconnection. When an individual was deemed somehow dangerous to scientology, then all scientologists were ordered to "disconnect" from that individual—that means, have nothing to do with him. Since scientology can often take up a large portion of an individual's life, a disconnection could mean that a person would abruptly lose most of his friends—a bruising experience.

The disconnection policy generated a great deal of unfavorable publicity for scientology. Finally in November 1968 this announcement appeared in the Public Notices of *The New York Times:* "The Church of Scientology wishes to make known that the policy know as disconnection is now ended. One individual no longer needs to separate from another." But disaffected scientologists report that their former friends still within the scientological orbit will not speak to them, and that the disconnection policy continues, though unofficially.

Hubbard and his great scientology invention leave one feeling distinctly uncomfortable. Perhaps this is unfair. Madame Blavatsky's flights of fancy were equally wild, and she was doubtless just as hard on her associates. She didn't make as much money as Hubbard has, but that is not because she didn't try. H.P.B.'s supersecret Esoteric Section, and Hubbard's Ethics Squad are almost carbon copies. One reason that H.P.B. seems almost lovable, and Hubbard distinctly disagreeable, is that she is dead, and well beyond causing any more mischief, and Hubbard is still very much alive.

But there is another reason. H.P.B. and most other mystics tried, in their own muddled way, to glorify man. Hubbard with his pseudo-technological jargon seems to seek to reduce the human race to a mass of cyphers. For all his talk of the goal of "Total Freedom," the true goal seems to be more of "Total Automation."

Today L. Ron Hubbard sits on his converted cattle boat surrounded by pictures and busts of himself, and served by a crowd of worshipful admirers. He talks, half-jokingly, of a red-haired messiah. (Hubbard has bright red hair.) What does he really believe? I don't know. I don't think anyone knows except L. Ron Hubbard himself, and perhaps he doesn't even know anymore.

CHAPTER X

Eileen Garrett

EILEEN GARRETT was never flashy or cheap.

Devotees of today's pop occultism who would recognize the names of Hans Holzer, Peter Hurkos, Jeane Dixon, Sybil Leak, and even Arthur Ford, might never have heard of Eileen Garrett. Yet among those seriously interested in psychic subjects, she is regarded as the greatest medium of the twentieth century, and one of the most important figures in the study of all forms of psychic phenomena.

I met Mrs. Garrett briefly, just a few weeks before her death in September 1970. I was one of the speakers at an International Conference of the Parapsychology Foundation. Mrs. Garrett was founder, president, and *raison d'être* for the Parapsychology Foundation. The conferences were held annually at a hotel near her villa in the South of France.

Mrs. Garrett was in her late seventies and quite ill. Severe arthritis had limited her movements to a few shuffling steps at a time, and the day I first met her she was barely able to rise from a chair without aid. She quickly pointed out that she was heavily drugged to kill the pain. This I later discovered was one of her good days.

After we were introduced she asked me about myself, and she listened with every indication of complete attention as I talked on aimlessly for about ten minutes. Then when I paused for a moment she said, "Thank you, Mr. Cohen, this has been so interesting." I had been dismissed, very politely but very definitely.

Yet I didn't feel insulted. I walked away with the feeling of how good it had been of this brave and noble woman to have spent any time with me at all. That was an odd and completely unexpected reaction.

I had gone to France with a preconceived notion of what the celebrated medium Eileen Garrett would be like. I had met other mediums and psychics, and found them an unimpressive, even sleazy lot. Mrs. Garrett turned out to be a long step above them in quality. I recalled the impressions of another reporter, who said after meeting Mrs. Garrett he felt like a snake that had been handled by an expert charmer.

As is usual in conferences, the participants spent a good deal of time sniping publicly and privately at one another. There were charges of idiocy, fraud, and insanity, as is usual when a group of people get together to discuss parapsychology. Naturally I sniffed around to see what I could find out about Mrs. Garrett. I found nothing bad. From the believers to the cynics everyone who knew her spoke of her in tones of respect, almost awe. I couldn't get anyone who knew her to say that she was anything other than an honest, kind, and generous woman. Not everyone seemed convinced she had psychic powers, but everyone said she was a good person.

I had never witnessed control exercised so subtly, yet so effectively over a group. Everything started and stopped according to Mrs. Garrett's needs, or whims. The atmosphere was what I imagine a royal court to have been like, in the days of absolute monarchy. And I found myself slipping easily and comfortably into the role of courtier.

A striking example of Mrs. Garrett's power was displayed after a paper written by Eric J. Dingwall was read. Dr. Dingwall is an old man, and was unable to attend the conference, but he is a longtime veteran and often gadfly of psychical research. Though he should be classed as a believer in the psychic, any number of fakers have been exposed by his investigations. Among other unpleasant things, Mr. Dingwall said that many reputable psychologists were not interested in parapsychology because they "do not want to be associated with the parapsychologists whose reputation for truth is not of the highest and who are linked with a crowd of dubious and half-baked seekers after marvels." His paper finished with the announcement that he was through with psychical research forever.

I was ready to jump up and yell, "Right on!" But everybody else just sat there in glum silence. After a few uncomfortable moments someone suggested that perhaps Mrs. Garrett might like to comment on the paper. She rose, smiled slightly, and said, "I've known Eric for years. He's such a naughty boy." Everybody laughed, and the dampening effect of Dr. Dingwall's paper was dissipated immediately. All the perfectly valid and uncomfortable criticisms were suddenly reduced to examples of Eric's naughtiness.

Several factors accounted for Mrs. Garrett's total control over this group of people. First, some were employees of the Parapsychology Foundation and some were doing work that in one way or another was funded by the Foundation. To be anything less than worshipful to the person who in reality was the Foundation might be financially suicidal.

Then, in fact, we were all Mrs. Garrett's guests at the conference. The setting was lovely, and the South of France was a place few of us would have been able to afford on our own. I for one was tortured by the fear that after my critical speech was delivered I would be handed my unpaid hotel bill as punishment.

Of course, there was also common decency. Mrs. Garrett was an old and very ill woman who was sitting bravely through all our long-winded speeches—she deserved respect.

But when I totaled all the factors I have outlined, something still seemed to be missing. Not fear, good manners, or common decency or a combination of the three could account for everyone's attitude toward Mrs. Garrett, including my own. She seemed to possess a power or quality of personality that immediately inspired trust and respect. I imagine many great leaders possess similar qualities. A popular term today is charisma, though this tends to imply screaming crowds. Personal magnetism is another popular descriptive term, but the history of mesmerism makes me rather unwilling to use that particular description. Whatever word or words one chooses to use, I believe that this sort of force of personality accounts for the remarkable accomplishments of many of the persons discussed in this book.

There is little mystery or deliberate mystification about Eileen Garrett's early life. She was born on March 17, 1893, in Beau Park, County Meath, Ireland. She was not the poor Irish country lass, fabled in legend. In the first place her mother, Anne Brownell, was not a Catholic, but a member of a strict Protestant family that had originally come from France. Nor was her family poor—they had at least enough money for her mother to be educated in Belgium. While visiting some French relatives in Algiers, Anne Brownell met a Spanish Basque named Vancho. She married him and was immediately ostracized by her family, who would never accept a Catholic son-in-law. Still, when she found she was going to have a baby, she and her husband returned to Ireland where her family lived. The reception the family gave her was not gracious. A few days after her baby was born, Anne Brownell-Vancho drowned herself. Six weeks later her husband also committed suicide, and the baby, Eileen Janette, was turned over to an aunt. The baby's name was changed and she was baptized in the (Protestant) Church of Ireland.

Though in her autobiographies, Mrs. Garrett treads ever so delicately around the subject, it is clear enough that her childhood was not a happy one, and she disliked her strict aunt.

Now the Irish countryside is the traditional home of the fairies, "the little people." The ability to see the little people is traditionally part of the equipment of Irish "sensitives." Did Eileen Garrett see fairies, or believe in them? Well, yes and no. "In my childhood I watched for them from dawn until the dew dried on the grass, and searched through the spring and summer twilights, never, alas, to find them. Still, when you have lived by the banks of the Boyne and wandered there in the long twilight, you cannot resist the conviction that you are not alone."

Though there were no fairies as such, Eileen did have "the Children," two girls and a boy who were her companions off and on from the time she was four years old. They were strange companions, for no one else could see them.

"The Children," she wrote, "taught me to watch changing expressions of anger, fear, and uncertainty in people's faces—

to listen to their voices and catch the meanings of varying tones and cadences." This sort of observation is very valuable to a medium.

She also shifted to "the Children" the blame for her youthful disobedience and willfulness, though she didn't quite put it that way. " 'The Children' taught me not to regard too seriously everything that grownups said, and finding my elders so often lacking in sympathy for the things that I knew to be true, I gathered courage to face the consequences of insisting that I was right."

School in Meath was bad for young Eileen, and transfer to a fashionable Protestant boarding school in Dublin actually made matters worse. She had never been a healthy child and at the age of fifteen Eileen suffered a complete physical breakdown. Her condition was ultimately diagnosed as latent tuberculosis, and the doctor suggested that she be sent to a drier climate. She was sent to London, which, though hardly dry, is drier than Ireland.

Eileen was lodged with some distant relatives, and was to enroll in school in London. However, not long after her arrival she met an architect named Clive Berry, and she married him, though she was still a teenager, and he was some twelve years her senior. The marriage was unhappy almost from the start. In one of her autobiographies, *Adventures in the Supernormal,* Mrs. Garrett speaks with uncharacteristic frankness of how shortly before the birth of her first child her husband had already returned to one of his former mistresses. Still a year later a second child was born to the couple. But within a few months both children died of meningitis.

The unsatisfactory marriage limped on, and a third child was born, but he survived only a few hours. Eileen's health continued to be bad, yet she had a fourth child, her first daughter and the first to survive to adulthood. When World War I broke out, the separations between Eileen and her husband grew longer and longer. Finally, after he began living openly with another woman, the marriage was ended officially.

Eileen married again. Her second husband was a young soldier who was killed a few weeks later. So she married again, just a few weeks before the armistice ending the war was signed. Her third husband was James William Garrett, a wounded soldier whom she had met at a hospital. Of this she wrote, "I confess I drifted into my third marriage without any thought of its being permanent." And indeed it was not, for this marriage too ended in divorce. The only permanent effect that it seemed to have on Eileen's life was that she kept the name Garrett.

During the war years, Mrs. Garrett opened a hostel for soldiers and proved herself to be an effective businesswoman —a talent that she was to display again and again in the future. She also began to mingle with some people in the arts, particularly theater people from the Abbey Theater whom she met on her occasional returns to Dublin, and with some of the intellectual socialists of the day.

Outwardly then Eileen Garrett seemed an unhappy and unlucky young woman, but one who was nevertheless intelligent, ambitious, and strong-willed. She quite clearly had no talent or desire to fit into the Victorian image of passive wife and mother. One is tempted to make a comparison between Mrs. Garrett and that other unconventional Victorian lady, Madame Blavatsky. But while H.P.B. attacked established society with a blunderbuss, Mrs. Garrett rebelled with more discretion. As I said, Eileen Garrett was never flashy or cheap. But both Madame Blavatsky and Mrs. Garrett chose the psychic path as the means by which they could get the recognition usually denied even very talented women by society. It has been said that mediumship was the second profession in which a woman might obtain power and influence.

Up until the days following World War I there seems to have been nothing particularly unusual about Mrs. Garrett's alleged psychic experiences. There were invisible playmates, but many isolated and imaginative persons have had similar experiences. She also claimed to have premonitions concerning the early death of her three sons, but what mother or father, for that matter, has not had such fearful premonitions about their children?

The first really startling psychic experience Eileen Garrett recorded came shortly after the war while her daughter was seriously ill. One night she heard a voice telling her to open the windows so that the child could breathe more freely. She obeyed the command and saw the figure of a man clad in gray garments. "He was smiling in a kindly, sympathetic way with a contagious sense of cheerfulness. I was reassured and knew that he had come to help me."

The child recovered, but afterwards Mrs. Garrett suffered one of her frequent collapses in health.

World War I had brought about a tremendous upsurge of interest in spiritualism, and the subject was widely discussed, particularly in the intellectual and artistic circles that Mrs. Garrett frequented. Mrs. Garrett expressed more than a passing interest in spiritualism and attended a number of seances. "One late afternoon I had allowed myself to sit down with a group of ladies who were seeking answers from the dead through the motions of a table. It was in a mood of indifferent politeness that I had allowed myself to participate. I was told afterward that an astonishing thing had happened during the session. It seems I went to sleep and began to speak of seeing the dead relatives of those at the table. Never before having witnessed such a phenomena, and being frightened, they shook me awake. I remember feeling rather uncomfortable. There were lights in front of my eyes, and I had a distinct feeling of nausea."

At the urging of her friends she went to see a theosophist who was deeply involved in the study of psychic subjects. Mrs. Garrett slipped easily into a trance. "On my awakening, the teacher informed me that he had spoken to one 'Uvani,' an entity or 'control' personality of Oriental origin, who foretold that I would become the vehicle for this type of work and that for a number of years I would serve in the capacity of trance medium."

Over her husband's objections she continued to explore the possibilities of her psychic self. Mrs. Garrett came under the influence of Hewat McKenzie and his wife, the founders of the British College of Psychic Science, and she worked with the McKenzies as a trance medium for ten years.

In 1923 she also met Eric Dingwall. "I was no newcomer on the psychic scene," he wrote. "I had been attending seances for some fifteen years. We became very friendly and I had a feeling that, if a genuine medium existed, she might very well be one."

Dingwall urged Mrs. Garrett to experiment with physical mediumship—that is, attempt to produce various physical phenomena, the ringing of bells, moving of objects, etc., by supernatural means. McKenzie, however, urged her to pursue the path of mental mediumship, and McKenzie won.

The fact that Mrs. Garrett chose to become a mental rather than a physical medium makes any assessment of her accomplishments extremely difficult. If one is skeptical about psychic phenomena, then one assumes that all physical phenomena produced by mediums are due to trickery and that physical mediums are conscious and deliberate frauds. In fact, when physical mediums have been closely investigated this has proved to be the case. The notable exception even as far as parapsychologists are concerned is D. D. Home, and, as we have seen, Home's record is hardly one to inspire great confidence in the ability and honesty of physical mediums. But, at least the physical medium produces something which can be measured, weighed, or otherwise tested. The mental medium presents the investigator with a much more subtle and difficult set of problems.

The mental medium does not claim to be able to produce any sort of information on demand. Thus the investigator cannot ask the medium to predict tomorrow's Dow Jones averages or the fall of a pair of dice. Nor can the investigator demand that the medium produce any exact piece of information from the alleged spirit of someone who has died. Most of the information produced by mental mediums during seances is of the most general nature. Much of it consists of moralistic sermons, and while some profess to find great comfort in such utterances they are absolutely worthless as far as scientifically establishing communication with the dead is concerned.

While the physical medium is either the genuine possessor of powers that we would have to call paranormal, or is a fraud, the mental medium may actually be neither. Mrs. Garrett had often wondered whether "Uvani" or the other "spirit controls" who apparently spoke through her when she was in a trance state were really the spirits of individuals who had died, or somehow fragments of her own personality. "I'm the greatest skeptic of all," she told me. "I just go to sleep and these things happen. I don't know whether they have any meaning at all."

Obviously it is extremely difficult to evaluate the claims to special powers of a person who makes no claims to special powers. But claims or no, Eileen Garrett soon developed the reputation of being one who could communicate with the dead, and who could supply the living with messages that would help them, and she profited greatly from this reputation.

For the ten years that she worked with McKenzie, there were few attempted tests of her reality of ability. McKenzie, who was thoroughly convinced of the reality of mediumistic phenomena, discouraged such tests. He was interested only in exploring the world of the spirits. He felt no need first to prove that such a world existed.

During this period Mrs. Garrett's life remained relatively tranquil. But after McKenzie's death a number of disruptions occurred in rapid succession. Her husband told her that he had found another woman, and wished a divorce—a request that Mrs. Garrett was quite willing to grant.

She also began using, or being used by, another control in addition to "Uvani." This new personality was "Abdul Latif," who claimed to have been a Persian physician and astronomer who had lived in the court of Saladin during the twelfth century. Most of "Abdul Latif's" messages concerned health or healing. "Abdul Latif" was already a fairly well-known control who had figured in the work of a number of other mediums.

Once again Mrs. Garrett contemplated remarrying. "Life was wonderful and everything progressed smoothly in this direction until the day when the banns of the marriage were announced. On that day both my fiance and I fell suddenly ill.

He having caught a chill, developed septic pneumonia, and I was taken to hospital with an active mastoid and ruptured appendix." Mrs. Garrett survived, her fiance did not.

In 1931, while still recovering from this illness, Mrs. Garrett received an invitation to visit the United States and work under the auspices of the American Society for Psychical Research in New York. After this first journey she spent an increasingly large percentage of her time in the United States and ultimately divided most of her time between New York and the south of France. In the United States her trance mediumship was studied by such luminaries in the psychical research field as William McDougall, Dr. Adolph Meyer, and Dr. Alexis Carrel. All were impressed by her apparent abilities.

Unfortunately the vast majority of these tests, like those conducted earlier by Hewat McKenzie, were not designed to test the existence of psychic powers—that was taken for granted. They were designed to measure, explore, or use these powers. Thus while the results seem enormously impressive to those already convinced of the existence of paranormal abilities, such tests seem vague, unduly complex, and downright foolish to those who still want to be shown that such powers exist in the first place.

The closest that parapsychologists have ever come to constructing a definitive series of tests of the powers they believe in, were the famous card guessing tests conducted by Dr. J. B. Rhine of Duke University. Most professional mediums resisted such tests of their abilities. Mrs. Garrett was one of the few who did not, but she didn't like them either. "I felt that Dr. Rhine's ESP cards lacked the energy stimulus which would enable me to see clairvoyantly their symbols. In fact, it would seem that the handling of the cards and their inanimate symbols inhibited, for the time being, whatever supernormal powers I possess."

Dr. Rhine believed that while Mrs. Garrett's scores were not spectacular, they were above chance and that she was far and away the best medium he had ever worked with. Mrs. Garrett thought that her scores on the clairvoyant tests—that is, attempting to see the cards at a distance—were no better than chance, while her telepathy scores—attempting to pick up the symbols by reading the mind of a person who was looking at the card—were somewhat better. "In the telepathy experiments, I was freed from direct concentration on the cards themselves and was able to receive the symbols from the mind of the transmitter, where they acquired vitality and provided the energy stimulus necessary for my perception."

In later years Mrs. Garrett seemed quite bitter about Rhine's tests, the publicity they had received, and the direction she felt that they had given to psychical research.

Because of her unrelieved bad health, Mrs. Garrett began to spend a lot of time in the friendly climate of southern France. She was there in 1940 when France fell, and was forced to leave, in rather a hurry. She came back to America, at that time a haven of peace and security in a war-torn world. In America, Mrs. Garrett, who had already had some success as a businesswoman, decided to go into the publishing business. She started the Creative Age Press, which published her own very popular books, as well as books by others mainly on psychic subjects. She also published *Tomorrow* magazine, more of a literary than a psychic magazine, which listed among its contributors such celebrated authors as Thomas Mann and Robert Graves.

Tomorrow survived as a literary magazine for about ten years, a goodly lifespan for such a venture. In 1951 *Tomorrow* was turned into a quarterly magazine devoted exclusively to psychic subjects, and this extended its life for another ten years, though Mrs. Garrett's book publishing firm—under a succession of different company names—continues to this day.

In 1951 Eileen Garrett established the Parapsychology Foundation, an organization devoted to sponsoring psychical research. Though by this time Mrs. Garrett was a fairly wealthy woman, she had nowhere near enough funds to support this sort of a foundation. Much of the money came from the Honorable Frances P. Bolton, a congressional representative from Ohio, who had the reputation for being the richest woman in Congress.

The Foundation sponsored all manner of research. Eric Dingwall complained bitterly about much of it. "I hated to see her [Mrs. Garrett] exploited by the many charlatans who are always holding out their begging bowls to generous souls who find it difficult to resist their flattering blandishments. It was but rarely that I succeeded in persuading her to refuse a grant to some patent swindler. After all, the Foundation was her brain child and I loved her for caring for it. 'You never know,' she used to say, 'there might be something and we mustn't miss it, must we?' "

Mrs. Garrett herself seemed to be the chief experimental subject for the Foundation researches. Her experiments ran the gamut from L.S.D. to voodoo. She has performed inside a Faraday cage to block electrical currents, with electrodes attached to her head to measure brain waves, and under the influence of a wide variety of drugs and in exotic settings. She might well have claimed the reputation of being the most tested woman in history.

She also traveled a good deal and, according to her associates, she was always being sought out by individuals who were looking for messages from dead friends, advice about the future, psychic diagnosis of illness, etcetera. Mrs. Garrett never played the part of common medium or fortune-teller, though she was occasionally supposed to have startled people with apparent messages from the dead or predictions about the future. Most often she gave people who came to her a sort of general spiritual guidance. I would very much like to have seen her at work.

Her books, while they are always vague, often sugary, and sometimes disconcertingly marred by name-dropping, are still far and away the best ever written by a modern "professional sensitive." One can read them without laughing out loud or getting angry. And one comes out of them with at least a small feeling of reassurance about the meaning and purpose of life. I suspect that in person she would have been able to convey this message much more forcefully.

What was Eileen J. Garrett? Her own judgment was this: "I have been called many things, from a charlatan to a miracle woman. I am, at least, neither of these."

One can quickly agree that she was no miracle woman. The various phenomena attributed to her, the glimpses of the future and the knowledge of things that could not have been gained by normal means, are the sort of stories that surround every professional psychic from carnival fortune-tellers on up. They are interesting, but hardly constitute hard evidence for any psychic powers, and I think Mrs. Garrett would agree.

Regarding the charge of charlatan, one cannot be so sure, not because there is any evidence that she faked any of the phenomena that are attributed to her, but simply because the entire field of mediumship has been so riddled with frauds that one hesitates to absolve any professional medium of the charge.

Still, she submitted herself quite openly, almost compulsively to tests. Admittedly most of the tests were not rigorous attempts to establish the reality of her powers. The only tests of that nature were Rhine's, and she didn't like them, or do very well. She was almost always in the hands of professional psychical researchers, and they do not have the best reputation for spotting frauds. Yet, there is a danger for the trickster in such tests, and a goodly number have been tripped up by psychical researchers. Remember what Richard Hodgson did to Madame Blavatsky. Most professional psychics choose to work with only a small number of "pet" researchers whom they are quite sure are stupid and blind or too crooked to expose their little tricks. In general, the professionals prefer to avoid any intensive examination of their alleged powers.

Mrs. Garrett certainly gave the strong impression of a woman genuinely puzzled by what she perceived to be her own abilities, and she spent a good part of her life trying to figure them out.

Only two other professional sensitives displayed a similar passion for being investigated. They were Mrs. Lenore Piper, and Mrs. Gladys Osborne Leonard, whose careers spanned the late nineteenth and early twentieth centuries. Both were mental mediums, and both produced the same sort of information that was produced by Mrs. Garrett.

Professor C. E. Hansel, who has been a persistent and influential critic of psychical research, has written: "There is a serious possibility that such mediums should be treated rather than investigated. The phenomena of mediumship is curiously summed up in a letter written by Mrs. Piper to the New York *Herald* on October 20, 1901. In it she denied that she was a spiritualist or had ever experienced any proof of spirit return. She then asked herself why she had remained with the Society for Psychical Research for so long and replied: 'Because of my desire to learn if I were possessed or obsessed.' "

In the end I would have to subscribe to Eric Dingwall's statement that Eileen Garrett was psychical research's "most striking and complex personality." Such a judgment is, I am quite aware, something of a cop-out, because it does not answer the question that immediately springs to everyone's mind—was she a real "psychic" or was she a phony. "Striking and complex" are ambiguous answers to such a straightforward question. I am also painfully aware that for nearly a century now a great deal of nonsense that has been passed off as psychical research has been kept afloat by just such ambiguous statements.

But given the nature of the powers that Mrs. Garrett claimed, it would be virtually impossible to establish hard and scientific evidence for their existence, and even more impossible to prove they did not exist. A great deal depends on whether one thinks Mrs. Garrett was an honest woman, and how deeply one believes or disbelives in psychic phenomena.

Unsatisfactory though they are, Eric Dingwall's "striking and complex" are the best descriptive adjectives I could come up with. Perhaps I might add "fascinating," as well.

SELECTED BIBLIOGRAPHY

Selected Bibliography

Besant, Annie W. *The Ancient Wisdom.* Adyar, India: Theosophical Publishing House, 1939.

Blavatsky, Helena. *Isis Unveiled* (2 vols). Point Loma, California: Theosophical University Press, 1877.

——. *The Secret Doctrine.* Adyar, India: Theosophical Publishing House, 1938.

Bouisson, M. *Magic, Its History and Principal Rites.* New York: E. P. Dutton, 1961.

Brown, Slater. *The Heyday of Spiritualism.* New York: Hawthorn Books, 1970.

Burland, C. A. *The Arts of the Alchemists.* New York: The Macmillan Co., 1967.

Burton, Joan. *Heyday of a Wizard.* New York: Alfred A. Knopf, 1944.

Cavendish, Richard. *The Black Arts.* New York: G. P. Putnam's Sons, 1967.

Christian, Paul. *The History and Practice of Magic.* New York: The Citadel Press, 1963.

Christopher, Milbourne. *ESP, Seers and Psychics, What the Occult Really Is.* New York: Thomas Y. Crowell Co., 1970.

——. *Houdini, the Untold Story.* New York: Thomas Y. Crowell Co., 1969.

——. *Panorama of Magic.* New York: Dover Publications, 1962.

Cohen, Daniel. *Mysterious Places.* New York: Dodd, Mead & Co., 1969.

——. *Myths of the Space Age.* New York: Dodd, Mead & Co., 1967.

——. *A Natural History of Unnatural Things.* New York: The McCall Co., 1971.

Daraul, Arkon. *A History of Secret Societies.* New York: The Citadel Press, 1962.

——. *Witches and Sorcerers.* New York: The Citadel Press, 1962.

Darnton, Robert. *Mesmerism and the End of the Enlightenment in France.* New York: Schocken Books, 1970.

Dauven, Jean. *The Powers of Hypnosis.* New York: Stein and Day, 1969.

De Camp, L. Sprague and Catherine. *Spirits, Stars and Spells.* New York: Canaveral Press, 1966.

De Giury, Grillot. *Witchcraft, Magic and Alchemy.* New York: Frederick, 1954.

Dingwall, Eric J. *Some Human Oddities.* London: Home and Van Thal, 1947.

—— and Hall, Trevor H. *Four Modern Ghosts.* London: Gerald Duckworth & Co., 1958.

Festinger, Leon; Riecken, Henry and Schachter, Stanley. *When Prophecy Fails.* Minneapolis: University of Minnesota Press, 1965.

Gardner, Martin. *Fads and Fallacies in the Name of Science.* New York: Dover Publications, 1957.

Garrett, Eileen J. *Adventures in the Supernormal.* New York: Garrett Publications, 1949.

——. *Awareness.* New York: Garrett Publications, 1943.

——. *Many Voices.* New York: G. P. Putnam's Sons, 1968.

——. *The Sense and Nonsense of Prophecy.* New York: Farrar, Straus and Giroux, 1950.

Gauld, Alan. *The Founders of Psychical Research.* New York: Schocken Books, 1968.

Glass, Justine. *They Foresaw the Future.* New York: G. P. Putnam's Sons, 1969.

Godwin, John. *This Baffling World.* New York: Hart Publishing Co., 1968.

Goldsmith, Margaret. *Franz Anton Mesmer.* New York: Doubleday, Doran, 1934.

Hall, Trevor H. *New Light on Old Ghosts.* London: Gerald Duckworth & Co., 1965.

——. *The Spiritualists.* New York: Helix Press, Garrett Publications, 1963.

Hansel, C. E. M. *ESP A Scientific Evaluation.* New York: Charles Scribners Sons, 1966.

Hill, Douglas and Williams, Pat. *The Supernatural.* New York: Hawthorn Books, 1966.

Hodgson, Richard. "Report of the Committee Appointed to Investigate Phenomena Connected With the Theosophical Society." in *Proceedings of the Society for Psychical Research, III,* London, 1885.

Holmyard, E. J. *Alchemy.* Baltimore: Penguin Books, 1968.

Home, Daniel Dunglas. *Incidents in My Life.* New York: Carleton, 1858.

———. *Lights and Shadows of Spiritualism.* New York: Carleton, 1877.

Home, Mme. Dunglas. *D. D. Home: His Life and Mission.* London: Kegan Paul, Trench, Trubner & Co., 1921.

Houdini, Harry. *Houdini on Magic.* New York: Dover Publications, 1963.

——— and Dunninger, J. *Houdini's Spirit World, Dunninger's Psychic Revelations.* New York: Tower Publications, 1970.

Hubbard, L. Ron. *Dianetics, the Modern Science of Mental Health.* New York: Hermitage House, 1950.

Hughes, Pennethorne. *Witchcraft.* Baltimore: Penguin Books, 1965.

Jastrow, Joseph. *Error and Eccentricity.* New York: Dover Publications, 1962.

Jennings, Gary. *Black Magic, White Magic.* New York: Dial Press, 1964.

Keel, John. *U.F.O.'s Operation Trojan Horse.* New York: G. P. Putnam's Sons, 1970.

Levi, E. *The History of Magic.* New York: E. P. Dutton, n.d.

Lewinsohn, Richard. *Science, Prophecy and Prediction.* New York: Harper & Brothers, 1961.

Lind, Ingrid. *Astrology and Commonsense.* London: Hodder & Stoughton, 1962.

Lyons, Arthur. *The Second Coming, Satanism in America.* New York: Dodd, Mead & Co., 1970.

MacDougall, Curtis. *Hoaxes.* New York: Dover Publications, 1958.

Mackay, Charles. *Extraordinary Popular Delusions and the Madness of Crowds.* Boston: L. C. Page & Co., 1932.

MacKenzie, Norman (editor). *Secret Societies.* New York: Holt, Rinehart & Winston, 1967.

McIntosh, Christopher. *The Astrologers and their Creed, An Historical Outline.* New York: Frederick A. Prager, 1969.

Malko, George. *Scientology, The Now Religion.* New York: Delacorte Press, 1970.

Mann, John. *Frontiers of Psychology.* New York: The Macmillan Co., 1963.

Mathison, Richard. *Faiths, Cults and Sects of America.* Indianapolis: Bobbs-Merrill Co., 1960.

Michelet, Jules. *Satanism and Witchcraft.* New York: The Citadel Press, 1939.

Nebel, Long John and Teller, Sanford. *The Psychic World Around Us.* New York: Hawthorne Books, 1969.

Podmore, Frank. *Mediums of the Nineteenth Century* (2 vols). New York: University Books, 1963.

Pratt, Joseph Gather. *Parapsychology, An Insider's View of ESP.* New York: E. P. Dutton, 1966.

Prince, Walter Franklin. *Noted Witnesses for Psychic Occurrences.* New York: University Books, 1963.

Rawcliffe, D. H. *Illusions and Delusions of the Supernatural and the Occult.* New York: Dover Publications, 1959.

Read, John. *Prelude to Chemistry, an Outline of Alchemy.* Cambridge, Mass.: The M.I.T. Press, 1966.

Rhine, J. B. *Extra Sensory Perception.* Boston: Bruce Humphries, 1964.

Rhine, Louisa E. *ESP in Life and Lab.* London: The Macmillan Co., 1967.

Rhodes, H. T. F. *The Satanic Mass.* London: Arrow books, 1964.

Robbins, Rossell Hope. *The Encyclopedia of Witchcraft and Demonology.* New York: Crown Publishers, 1959.

Rohmer, Sax. *The Romance of Sorcery.* New York: Paperback Library, 1970.

Scott, Sir Walter. *Letters on Demonology and Witchcraft.* New York: Ace Books, 1970.

Seligmann, K. *History of Magic.* New York: Pantheon, 1948.

Seth, Ronald. *Witches and Their Craft.* New York: Taplinger, 1968.

Shah, Idries. *The Secret Lore of Magic.* New York: The Citadel Press, 1958.

Sinnett, A. P. *Incidents in the Life of Madame Blavatsky.* London: Theosophical Publishing Society, n.d.

Smith, Eleanor Touhey. *Psychic People.* New York: William Morrow & Co., 1968.

Solovyoff, Vsevold Sergyevich. *A Modern Priestess of Isis.* London: Longmans, Green, 1895.

Spence, Lewis. *An Encyclopedia of Occultism.* New York: Dodd, Mead & Co., 1920.

Spraggett, Allan. *The Unexplained.* New York: The New American Library, 1967.

Stearn, Jess. *The Door to the Future.* New York: Doubleday, 1963.

Summers, Montague. *The Geography of Witchcraft.* New York: University Books, n.d.

——. The History of Witchcraft and Demonology. New York: University Books, 1956.

——. A Popular History of Witchcraft. London: Kegan Paul, Trench, Trubner, 1937.

Van Over, Raymond. *ESP and the Clairvoyants.* New York: Award Books, 1970.

West, D. J. *Psychical Research Today.* London: Gerald Duckworth Co., 1967.

Williams, Gertrude Marvin. *Madame Blavatsky, Priestess of the Occult.* New York: Alfred A. Knopf, 1946.

INDEX

Index